When Nothing Else Works

What Early Childhood Professionals Can Do to Reduce Challenging Behaviors

By William DeMeo, PhD

DEDICATION

This book is dedicated to young children and their families. I hope that its contents will assist early childhood professionals in meeting the unique needs of those under their guidance and in empowering them to reach their full potential.

ACKNOWLEDGEMENTS

I am indebted to all the young children, families, and early childhood professionals I have worked with in the past 30 years. They have influenced my development as a psychologist and have ignited my passion to educate.

Special thanks to Jodi Perry and Laura Laxton for their relentless dedication and perseverance in reading and editing this publication. Their ongoing support and encouragement throughout this journey have assisted in the formation of this work.

Finally, a salutation to my wonderful wife, Beth; my twin sons, Nicholas and Nathaniel; and my daughter, Natalie: You have given me a salubrious perspective on being a husband, a father, an educator, and a psychologist.

Early Childhood Education

WHEN NOTHING ELSE WORKS

What Early Childhood Professionals Can Do to Reduce Challenging Behaviors

WILLIAM DEMEO, PHD

Gryphon House, Inc.
Lewisville, NC

LIBRARY OF CONGRESS CATALOGING-IN-PUBLICATION DATA

The Cataloging-in-Publication Data is registered with the Library of Congress for ISBN 978-0-87659-480-3.

BULK PURCHASE

Gryphon House books are available for special premiums and sales promotions as well as for fund-raising use. Special editions or book excerpts also can be created to specifications. For details, contact the director of marketing at Gryphon House.

DISCLAIMER

Gryphon House, Inc., cannot be held responsible for damage, mishap, or injury incurred during the use of or because of activities in this book. Appropriate and reasonable caution and adult supervision of children involved in activities, and corresponding to the age and capability of each child involved, are recommended at all times. Do not leave children unattended at any time. Observe safety and caution at all times.

Table of Contents

WHEN NOTHING ELSE WORKS

PREFACE

Reducing challenging behaviors is a team effort. For interventions of challenging behaviors to have the highest level of success, major stakeholders, including directors, teachers, parents, and other possible professionals such as mental health consultants, speech-language pathologists, health coordinators, nutrition coordinators, and occupational therapists, must collaborate. Through collaboration—sharing different areas of expertise and responsibility while working toward common goals—you will have success in achieving what is in the best interest of the child.

Families want what is best for their child and have valuable knowledge about the child that is vital in developing the most practical and effective interventions. For example, parents may be able to provide crucial details about the child's development, birth and health history, temperament, sleeping patterns, eating habits, and interests that may not be transparent to staff members. These details may provide insights into the function of the child's behavior. Working with a child's family is always a better idea than just coming up with prevention and intervention strategies on your own. When the family is involved, they are more likely to be supportive and to help implement the specific strategies at home that will affect behavior. Remember that most families know their child best. Work with them to highlight the child's abilities, interests, and behaviors.

WHEN NOTHING ELSE WORKS

INTRODUCTION

Years ago, when I was completing my school-psychologist internship, a sixth-grade teacher gave me the following story written by one of her students, and she asked me what I thought.

BEAVER THE CLEAVER

Hey Wally, shouted Beaver do you want to play a game? No, Beaver I have better things to do than play with you, you little toothless brat! I'm going to go upstairs with my girlfriend you little scum! I'm going outside to get some friends for a party you go outside and play with your friends! Shut up, Wally, you know mom doesn't want you to talk to me like that, the doctor says I'm mentally sick! Oh shut up you, retarded hill-bred flea-bitten scum bag! Now go play in your sandbox or go play on the highway. While the party is going on, Wally does not note that Beaver has been in the bathroom all night. Suddenly, the door burst open and with a small assortment of butcher knives on his belt, a machete on his hip, an axe in his left hand, and an cleaver in his right. All of sudden he takes the cleaver and hacks Wally's girlfriend in a shower of her own blood! He doesn't stop, pieces of flesh and organs cover the floor, then he shouts at Wally, I told you I'm sick, now you want forget it. Blindly Joe lunges at Beaver for the murder weapon but Beaver is too agile and hacks off his left arm off as blood spurts in the air. Beaver finishes the gory job with the bloody axe. Beaver repeats after his favorite cartoon character: That's not all folks and then he throws a butcher knife at Sue and it lands in her chest with a bloody spurt she falls stone dead on the floor. Relentlessly Beaver picks up the cleaver and the razor-sharp murder weapon becomes a flying guillotine and savagely slices his head. Stay tune for the next issue.

You might be wondering why I chose to feature this troubling story, written by an older child, in a book focused on young children's behavior. I wanted to emphasize a very important point: Behavior becomes more challenging as children mature. In the case of this student, when our research team began its case study, we discovered that he had attended one of the preschool programs within the district years earlier. It turns out that during his preschool experience he displayed challenging behaviors. The response of his teacher at the time? "He will outgrow it."

Research has shown that children do not outgrow this type of behavior—rather, the behavior becomes even more challenging as they mature. The earlier you intervene, the more successful the interventions will be. This book will provide you with knowledge and skills you can use to help these children.

It is my sincere wish that this book provides a beacon of hope to both educators and families who are feeling lost or frustrated on a daily basis as they interact with children who exhibit disruptive behaviors. My years as a teacher made me aware that many educators struggle with children who have challenging behaviors. I earned my graduate degree in psychology so I could help children and become a resource for families and education professionals. I have spent 25 years providing psychological services to children who have mental health concerns, and I want to share the strategies I have learned to help teachers, families, and—most importantly—children succeed and develop to their fullest potential.

Most of the books addressing challenging behaviors in young children are written by early childhood professionals, administrators, educators, or researchers. This book is written from the perspective of a developmental school psychologist. From my years collaborating with educators and parents to prevent and intervene with persistent challenging behaviors exhibited in early childhood settings, I have recognized the enormous need for additional skills and strategies that address these behaviors when nothing else works. Most books offer guidance and discipline strategies for troubled young children. Built on a strong foundation of developmentally appropriate practice, this book provides skills, strategies, and—hopefully—solutions for educators and families who feel like they have run out of options.

Incorporating the latest research regarding prevention and intervention, this book also explores the constructs that are essential to addressing extreme challenging behavior: growth mindset, social and emotional intelligence, resiliency, and advances in the field of neuroscience. Educators and families will learn why, when, and how to implement strategies and skills that prevent and intervene with a child's disruptive behavior.

I provide **specific answers** to common questions about behavior–answers grounded in research and evidenced-based practices that lead to practical and effective strategies for dealing with those behaviors.

- You will learn about the key variables associated with behavior, such as *antecedents* (triggers) and *consequences.*
- You will gain ideas and strategies for structuring the classroom environment, clearly communicating class routines and expectations, and cultivating a growth mindset that will prepare you to address the challenging behavior young children might display.
- You will learn strategies for developing key components of *social and emotional intelligence,* including self-regulation, recognizing feelings in self and others, calming oneself when upset, social awareness, and developing relationships.
- You will learn how to collect data on a child's behavior, including such critical elements as *frequency, intensity, duration,* and *latency,* to determine if behavior is improving.
- You will learn more about resiliency in children and ways to develop the important protective factors associated with the social and emotional intelligences that can alter or even reverse expected negative outcomes.

Even with all of the developmentally appropriate practices in place to prevent and intervene with challenging behavior, some children will still exhibit disruptive behavior in your program. This book provides creative strategies to use when nothing else works and provides guidance in pulling together this wealth of information to develop an intervention plan to be used not only by your program but also by the families.

In my years of experience working with children who exhibit persistent, extreme challenging behavior, I've seen tremendous positive change in these children. If you are faced with challenging behavior and you see no end in sight, I invite you to join me on this journey of hope. So, get ready to color outside the lines and push the boundaries of what you know and have tried, especially when nothing else works.

11

12

1

BRAIN BASICS

What is the relationship between the brain and behavior? During the past few decades, an explosive growth of knowledge in the cognitive sciences has begun to yield answers to fundamental mysteries about the nature of human behavior. The scientific and medical communities have made great strides in answering the question of how physical matter (the brain) relates to mental phenomena such as perception, memory, learning, attention, and behavior. The study of that relationship resides primarily in the field of cognitive neuroscience.

Cognitive neuroscience takes a multidisciplinary approach to the study of the brain and human behavior, studying internal mental processes and the chemistry, physiology, and anatomy of neurons and neural systems. It provides the latest advances in how human behavior is connected to the brain, which helps us understand how behavior works physiologically. This, in turn, enables us to design interventions and behavior adaptations based on the brain mechanisms involved.

A child learns as a single, integrated organism. To the brain, everything is one complex, adaptive system that creates and controls information. All learning depends on the body's physiological state. Each posture and movement stores a separate library of learning; for example, eye movements trigger visual, auditory, and kinesthetic senses. It is natural, right, and normal for a child to want to explore whatever objects are within his reach, especially those he has not explored before. Individuals gain more skills by active participation than they do by passive participation.

Each person's brain differs from all other brains in the world. This uniqueness can be explained by the genetic makeup of the brain and the environmental influences that mold the individual's personality, character, learning style, and emotional system. Because these factors differ from person to person, we should avoid gender, age, and classroom comparisons. The method that makes the most sense is comparing a child to himself over time.

How the Brain Functions

The brain is part of the central nervous system and controls many bodily functions, both voluntary and involuntary. The adult brain weighs about three pounds and contains mostly water (78 percent), fat (10 percent), and protein (8 percent). The brain has two hemispheres, and each hemisphere has four lobes. Each of these lobes has numerous folds, which do not mature at the same time. The chemicals that foster brain development are released in waves—as a result, areas of the brain evolve in a predictable sequence. This explains, in part, why there are "prime times" for certain kinds of learning and development.

The two hemispheres are connected by bundles of nerve fibers, the largest of which is known as the corpus callosum. The corpus callosum has about 250 million nerve fibers and allows each side of the brain to exchange information freely.

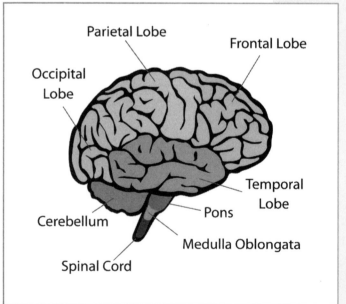

WHEN NOTHING ELSE WORKS

The four lobes are the *occipital, frontal, parietal,* and *temporal.* The occipital lobe is in the middle rear area of the brain and is responsible for vision. The frontal lobe is the area around the forehead and is involved with purposeful acts such as judgment, creativity, problem solving, and planning. The parietal lobe is the top rear area of the brain and is responsible for processing higher sensory and language functions. The temporal lobes (left and right side) are above and around the ears. Their duties include hearing, memory, meaning, and language.

In addition, different parts of the brain control various functions:

- **Amygdala:** Located in the middle of the brain, this almond-shaped complex is a critical processing area for the senses. Connected to the hippocampus, it plays a role in emotionally laden memories. The amygdala contains a huge number of opiate receptor sites, which have a role in rage, fear, and sexual feelings.
- **Basal Ganglia:** These clusters of nuclei deep within the cerebrum and the upper parts of the brain stem play an important part in producing smooth, continuous muscular actions for stopping and starting movement.
- **Brain Stem:** Located at the top of the spinal cord, it links the lower brain with the middle of the brain and the cerebral hemispheres. It is responsible for breathing, heart rate, and blood pressure.
- **Cerebellum:** A cauliflower-shaped structure located below the occipital area and next to the brain stem. The Latin word means "little brain." It is linked to balance, posture, coordination, and muscle movements, as well as cognition, novelty, and emotions. Research also suggests strong links between the cerebellum and memory, spatial perception, language, attention, emotion, nonverbal cues, and decision making. The cerebellum takes up just one-tenth of the brain by volume, but it contains more than half of all the brain's neurons. It has some 40 million nerve fibers that feed information between the cortex and the cerebellum.
- **Cerebrum:** The largest part of the brain, composed of the left and right hemispheres, it contains the frontal, parietal, temporal, and occipital lobes.
- **Hippocampus:** Found deep in the temporal lobe, central to the middle of the brain area and connected to the amygdala, this crescent-shaped area is strongly involved in learning and memory formation.
- **Hypothalamus:** Located in the bottom center of the middle of the brain, under the thalamus, this complex, thermostat-like structure

influences and regulates appetite, hormone secretion, digestion, sexuality, circulation, emotions, and sleep.

A *neurotransmitter* is a substance that transmits nerve impulses, and different types of cells secrete different neurotransmitters. Each brain chemical works over widely spread areas and brain locations and may have a different effect depending on where it is activated. See Figure 1.1 for a list of important neurotransmitters and their functions.

FIGURE 1.1 KEY NEUROTRANSMITTERS

- **Dopamine:** Controls arousal levels in many parts of the brain and is vital for giving physical motivation. When levels are severely depleted—as in Parkinson's disease—a person may find it impossible to move forward voluntarily. Low dopamine may also be implicated in mental status. Hallucinogenic drugs are thought to work on the dopamine system.
- **Serotonin:** Has a profound effect on mood and anxiety; high levels of it are associated with serenity and optimism. It also affects sleep, pain, appetite, and blood pressure.
- **Acetylcholine:** Controls activity in brain areas connected with attention, learning, and memory.
- **Noradrenaline:** Induces physical and mental arousal and heightens mood. Production is centered in an area of the brain called the *locus coeruleus,* which is one of several candidates for the brain's pleasure center.
- **Glutamate:** The brain's major excitatory neurotransmitter, it is vital for forging the links between neurons that are the basis of learning and long-term memory.
- **Enkephalins and Endorphins:** Modulate pain, reduce stress, and promote a sensation of floaty, oceanic calm. They also depress physical functions such as breathing and may produce physical dependence.

PRINCIPLES OF BRAIN DEVELOPMENT

The beginning of brain development starts soon after conception and continues throughout the prenatal period. During pregnancy, the fetal nervous system produces several hundred billion nerve cells; however, one-third to one-half of these cells will disappear as the child develops. It is believed this "downsizing" is a necessary adjustment or refinement in the developmental process. With only a few specialized exceptions, no more nerve cells are added to the nervous system over the entire life span. Unlike the tissue in most other organs, each surviving nerve cell lives for the entire life of a healthy individual.

At birth, the infant's brain has one hundred billion nerve cells (also called *neurons*). These neurons will grow and connect with other neurons in systems that control functions such as seeing, hearing, moving, and expressing emotion. These systems, activated by repeated experiences, provide the foundation for the brain's organization and functioning throughout a person's life. If a child does not have these experiences, the absence of appropriate activation results in a lack of development or the disappearance of these connections.

At the same time neurons disappear, *dendrites*—the branches of nerve cells—increase, adding substantially to the surface area available for connections among cells. During a child's early years, the number of her synaptic connections might triple or quadruple, reaching levels of connectivity that may never be equaled again. By the age of 10, the number of synaptic connections begins to drop and continues to decline slowly as the child becomes an adult.

At birth, the brain is remarkably unfinished. The parts of the brain that handle thinking and remembering, as well as emotional and social behavior, are very undeveloped. The fact that the brain matures in the world rather than in the uterus means that early experiences deeply affect young children. Relationships with parents and other important caregivers; the sights, sounds, smells, and feelings they encounter; and the challenges they meet affect the way children's brains become wired. In other words, early experiences help determine brain structure, thus shaping the way a person learns, thinks, and behaves for the rest of her life.

Neuroscience research has shown that learning self-regulation is a primary task of newborns and is possible only in nurturing relationships. By providing appropriate and changing stimulation in response to a baby's states, moods, and interests, families and caregivers help the baby manage his level of arousal and build the networks for self-regulation.

When a baby is born, the brain is relatively undeveloped, with few emotional circuits and little or no ability to control them. A baby learns control from those who have it. In nurturing relationships, a baby's family or caregivers provide an environment and experiences that build pathways of neural connections through one-on-one stimulus and response. If this process is interrupted, for example, by stress, hunger, or the caregiver's inadequate responses, the neural connections may not be strong, compromising the child's ability to self-regulate.

CHAPTER 1 ■ BRAIN BASICS

- Be warm, loving, and responsive.
- Respond to the child's cues and clues.
- Talk, read, and sing to the child.
- Establish routines and rituals.
- Encourage safe exploration and play.
- Make TV watching selective and infrequent.
- Use discipline as an opportunity to teach instead of to punish.
- Recognize that each child is unique.
- Take care of yourself.

OUR ADAPTABLE BRAINS

Every brain adapts to its environment based on experience. Effective teaching and impactful change involve consideration of the entire complex system.

- Different areas of the brain develop and mature at different speeds. Individuals develop their "fight-or-flight" capacity first and their problem-solving skills last.
- Most areas of the brain are accessed daily. This happens because an individual's brain has already pruned away the neurons it does not need. A person's brain has been customizing itself since the day she was born. It has been designed to fit her life so naturally that it grows to the size she needs. The more she uses it, the more it expands.
- The brain is highly adaptive, especially in the early years of life. Severe damage to one hemisphere usually can be compensated for by the other hemisphere if the damage occurs early (before age five). After that, the ability to switch over is reduced.
- The brain alters its receptor sites for neurotransmitters based on the environment. In an excessively stressed or threatening situation, the brain will increase receptor sites for noradrenaline, which may result in more aggressive, impulsive behaviors.

Every brain develops in its own unique world and adapts in response to its environment. As a result, each brain modifies itself in response to things that others have not had to adapt to; it is the adaptation that makes us intelligent. Single-answer, one-way learning and testing make little sense. Humans have survived by problem-solving and flexible thinking.

Early childhood programs can encourage and support this necessary adaptation through offering children lots of open-ended explorations. Children's brains keep growing as long as teachers provide them with novel experiences, learner-controlled feedback, and appropriate challenges.

Researcher Marian Diamond discovered the malleability of the brain—its amazing ability to grow new connections with environmental stimulation. Her research found that when the environment is enriched, the brain develops a thicker cortex, more nerve branching, more growth spines, and larger cell bodies. This means the neurons communicate better with one another. Harold Chugani found that the school-age brain almost glows with energy consumption, burning 225 percent of the adult levels of glucose. The brain nearly explodes with spectacular growth during the early school years. During this time, stimulation, repetition, and novelty are essential to laying the foundations for later learning. According to William Greenough, the most critical ingredient to enrich the learner's brain is that the learning challenges the learner with new information or experiences. Also, there must be some way to learn from the experience through interactive feedback. Novelty can take the form of a change in the decor on the classroom walls every two or four weeks; change in instructional strategies; and use of computers, groups, field trips, guest speakers, pairings, games, student teaching, journaling, or multiage projects.

Challenge is important—too much and students will give up; too little and students will get bored. Mental challenge can come from new material, increasing the degree of difficulty of activities, or limiting the resources. This includes varying time, materials, access, expectations, or support in the learning process. The second component of enrichment is to maximize learner feedback. Feedback reduces uncertainty, increases coping abilities, and lowers the pituitary-adrenal stress responses. The brain itself is exquisitely designed to operate on feedback, both internal and external.

In the early childhood environment there are numerous opportunities for young children to receive feedback, which can be provided by the adults or the other children in the learning center. For example, if a child enters into the personal space of another child who is building an elaborate structure, the second child may say, "Be careful; you might knock down my building." The statement provides feedback to the first child about his actions. There also are software programs that provide

CHAPTER 1 ■ BRAIN BASICS

feedback to young children regarding their responses to specific activities or problems. Closed-ended materials provide immediate feedback to young children since the materials can only be assembled in a specific way; the finished product provides the feedback. Finally, visual cues or pictures of children engaging with materials that are posted in the environment can provide learners with specific cues about the intended use of materials. For example, a picture can show children building with the blocks instead of throwing them.

BIOLOGICAL FACTORS OF ATTENTION

Now that you have an understanding of the complexity of the brain, how it functions, and how it develops, let us focus on one of the most vital specific functions in the frontal cortex: attention. Attention has a tremendous impact not only on learning but also on behavior. I have heard—on more than one occasion—early childhood professionals ask questions such as, "Why can't this child be attentive?"

From a biological point of view, attention has two purposes: to promote survival and to extend pleasurable states. The brain is always paying attention to something; survival depends upon it. Children can be attentive in an educational environment when the learning is relevant,

engaging, and chosen by the learner. Attention can be external or internal, focused or diffused, vigilant, or relaxed:

- **External attention:** The child is drawn to novel objects or materials that she has not seen the classroom on previous occasions.
- **Internal attention:** The child makes a conscious decision to be attentive to auditory or visual stimulation.
- **Focused attention:** The child concentrates on one specific dimension of the stimuli, such as a car that she moves back and forth on the floor.
- **Diffuse attention:** The child focuses on the car and thinks of creative uses of and for it. Diffuse attention is inclusive and considered to be three-dimensional, giving equal attention to all internal and external stimuli simultaneously as well as the space, silence, and timelessness in which they occur.
- **Vigilance** (also referred to as *sustained attention*): The child remains alert to stimulus events.
- **Relaxed attention:** The child reduces the amount of attention she gives to something.

Selective attention depends on suppression of irrelevant data, such as ignoring the sound of the air conditioner or the buzz of the fluorescent lights, and the application of relevant data, such as listening to a favorite song or experiencing the texture of fingerpaint. This affirms the value of focused learning time followed by diffused activities such as reflection (LaBerge, 1995).

Once a child has sustained focused attention on a particular stimulus or piece of information, he needs to use diffused attention to reflect on the information so he can make sense of what he has observed and incorporate the concept into his previous knowledge base to make it meaningful to him.

If you want attention,

---

provide a strong contrast from what you were just doing.

Children can sustain focused attention for short periods, but it is not developmentally appropriate to expect them to focus for long periods. The human brain is poor at maintaining nonstop sustained attention, and after sustained attention, the brain needs time for processing and resting. Generally, the ability to sustain focused attention increases with age. Here are some general guidelines for developmentally appropriate expectations:

- **Five to seven years old:** 5-7 minutes of sustained attention
- **Eight to twelve years old:** 8-12 minutes of sustained attention
- **Thirteen to eighteen years old:** 13-15 minutes of sustained attention

Throughout the day, children have natural highs and lows in their ability to pay focused attention. Called *ultradian rhythms,* these are key cycles in the brain that last about 90-110 minutes. Each individual has about 16 cycles in a 24-hour period. Children who are consistently drowsy may be at the bottom of their attention cycle. Movements such as stretching and breathing can help focus attention; so if a child is drowsy, quietly encourage her to stand and stretch.

Because the brain shifts its cognitive abilities on those high and low cycles, assessments compiled over time, such as portfolios, are more inclusive and more accurate than one-shot tests. There's a change of blood flow and breathing during these ultradian cycles that affects learning (Klein, Pilon, Prosser, and Shannahoff-Khalsa, 1986). This oscillation suggests children will score lower if they are tested at the wrong time.

Why Young Children Need Processing Time

The brain does not maintain continuous, high-level attention for long periods. LaBerge's research suggests that our short attention spans evolved to allow us to react quickly to predators and prey and to let us update priorities by rechoosing the object of our attention. Because the brain does not do well maintaining very focused attention for long stretches of time, focused learning time should be followed by defined activities, such as reflection. After learning new information, the brain needs time to absorb and assimilate it.

In the classroom, there are three reasons why constant attention is counterproductive. First, much of what we learn cannot be processed consciously; it happens too fast. We need time to process. Second, to create new meaning, we need internal time. Meaning is always generated from within, not from without. Third, after each new learning experience, we need time for the learning to "imprint."

Learning happens when we turn our attention from external stimuli and let our brains have time to link new information with what we already know. Research suggests that we may want to allow for several minutes of reflection time after new learning. Teachers can encourage personal processing time after children learn new material, so the children have an opportunity to assimilate their new knowledge.

For example, when the teacher introduces the children to a geometrical design such as a circle, some children may not have prior knowledge of the concept. Once the concept is introduced, a reflection activity may help children associate items in their environment that are shaped like a circle, such as tires, Hula-Hoops, a cup, or a ring.

Discussing the new learning in small groups helps children assimilate new information into memory. Cramming more content per minute or moving from one piece of learning to the next guarantees that little will be learned or retained. How much time should be spent processing depends on the difficulty of the material and background of the learner. Teaching heavy and new content to novice learners may require a processing time of 2–5 minutes every 10–15 minutes. But the review of old material to well-rehearsed learners may require only a minute or so every 20 minutes.

Teachers can offer children a few minutes of processing time during or after story time, for example. Children often encounter new concepts in story books. Teachers can provide opportunities to process these new concepts by leading a discussion of how the concepts relate to the children, asking the children to role-play key concepts from the story, or having children draw a picture of events in the story.

THE ROLE OF EMOTIONS IN LEARNING

Emotions, thinking, and learning are all linked. Emotions drive attention, create meaning, have their own memory pathways, and help focus the mind and set priorities. Emotions affect children's behavior because they create distinct mind-body states. A *state* is a moment comprising a specific posture, breathing rate, and chemical balance in the body. An example of an arousal state would be when a child has been involved in a physical conflict with another child and becomes angry because she feels threatened. A calm, alert state can occur when the teacher has engaged the children in a series of relaxation activities, such as breathing, progressive relaxation, or stretching. The children are then ready to listen attentively.

The brain operates like a gland: It produces hormones, is bathed in them, and is run by them. Emotions trigger the chemical changes that alter our moods, behaviors, and eventually, our lives.

Individuals remember that which is most emotionally laden because the brain is overstimulated when strong emotions are present. In the classroom, feel free to show enthusiasm and excitement and to model a love of learning. The children will catch your enthusiasm and will be excited, too. Bring something exciting to class. Build suspense. Use a simile, tell a true emotional story, show a new item, read a book, or bring an animal. Let students know what excites you. This will make an impression on the children, and they will retain the information more easily. We remember information better when our brains are stimulated.

EFFECTS OF ANGER ON BEHAVIOR

Of all the emotions, anger has the most significant effect on children's behavior. Neuroscience research clearly demonstrates that four components—physiology, emotion, expression, and understanding—create the mind-body state in young children.

THE PHYSIOLOGICAL STATE

The perception of a threat, whether physical or symbolic, triggers a limbic surge. The body releases adrenaline, generating a rush of energy that lasts for minutes. Adrenaline readies the body for a good fight or quick flight, depending on how the emotional brain sizes up the opposition.

The emotional brain can stay alert and aroused for hours. Called the *cortical excitation stage,* this hair-trigger condition created by perceived threat lowers the threshold for what produces anger, explaining why people are more quick to anger if they already have been provoked or irritated by something else. For example, before coming to preschool in the morning, a child has an argument with his parent about what to wear. Even though the adrenal surge has run its course and the child appears calm when he arrives at school, the cortical excitation stage has been activated. When his preschool teacher says, "Good morning. Please hang up your coat," the child flies into a fit of rage. When a teacher is confronted with this type of situation, he often will report, "I don't know why the child went off like that."

THE EMOTIONAL STATE

The universal trigger for anger appears to be a sense of endangerment, which can take the form of an outright physical threat or of a symbolic threat to self-esteem or dignity. For young children, this symbolic threat may consist of being treated unjustly or rudely, being insulted or demeaned, or being frustrated in pursuing an important goal. For example, if a young child has to wait her turn to play on the computer or struggles to zip her coat because she has not developed the fine motor dexterity to accomplish that goal, she may become angry and frustrated.

THE EXPRESSION OF ANGER

Anger can be expressed in multiple ways, and educators might observe one or more of the following coping strategies in their classrooms:

- **Physical/verbal aggression:** Most young children display their anger through aggression by physically or verbally retaliating against the provocateur.
- **Venting:** Some children "get the anger out" by hitting; teachers can suggest they hit something such as a pillow or an inflatable punching bag. The idea of offering a child a substitute target for aggressive behavior is highly popular and may appeal to some teachers as an immediate response for a challenging situation; however, it is only a momentary diversion and does not teach the child to manage her anger.
- **Active resistance:** Some children physically or verbally defend their position, self-esteem, or possessions in nonaggressive ways.

25

- **Avoidance:** Some children express anger through avoidance or through attempts to escape the provocateur.
- **Adult seeking:** Some children seek the teacher for comfort or support or to tell the teacher what happened.
- **Verbal expression:** Although some children can express their anger, feelings, and needs through clear and assertive verbal expression, many children cannot. It should be the goal of all early childhood professionals to help children develop that ability to the fullest.

UNDERSTANDING EMOTION

As discussed in the book *The Socialization of Emotions,* edited by Michael Lewis and Carolyn Saarni, people can only understand an emotion when they pay attention to it. There are some basic cognitive processes that can help:

- **Memory:** Children who have developed unhelpful ways to express anger can revert to those strategies even after teachers have taught a more helpful perspective. This means teachers probably will have to remind children multiple times about the positive ways to express anger.
- **Language:** Talking about and labeling emotions helps children better understand their feelings. Help children understand anger by developing a vocabulary to label the emotion. Most children are aware of the correspondence between facial expressions and words to describe a feeling; however, they still may need to learn to label their emotions.
- **Self-regulatory behaviors:** Around the age of two, children begin to develop the capacity to self-regulate: control impulses, tolerate frustration, postpone gratification, and start or stop doing something even if the child does not want to do so. As children age, they are better able to use certain strategies to regulate their own behavior. The development of self-regulatory behaviors sets the stage for understanding and managing emotions, including anger.

Children's self-control is critical for learning, responsibility, and relationships. Self-control cuts across all domains of behavior and is a key feature of effective learning and creating and maintaining positive relationships. Self-regulation is a process of executive function, which is ranked by early childhood experts as the most critical aspect of school readiness and is directly linked to academic achievement and social and emotional development. Unfortunately, research has found that more than half of children entering school do so without sufficient levels of social-emotional and cognitive self-regulation.

EFFECTS OF STRESS ON NEUROLOGICAL DEVELOPMENT

Excessive stress and threats in the environment may be the single greatest contributor to children's impaired learning and development. When children are stressed—that is, faced by physical or symbolic danger—their adrenal glands release a substance called *cortisol*, which is also known as the "stress hormone." This triggers a string of physical reactions, including depression of the immune system, tensing of the large muscles, blood clotting, and increased blood pressure. Chronically high cortisol levels lead to the death of brain cells in the hippocampus, an area critical to explicit memory formation.

CONNECTION BETWEEN BRAIN INJURY AND CHALLENGING BEHAVIORS

Managing difficult behaviors after pediatric brain injury presents a challenge. Although many areas of the brain can influence behavior, the two areas most often injured are the frontal and temporal lobes.

The frontal lobes help regulate the seat of emotions, contained in the limbic system of the brain. When frontal-lobe damage occurs or the connection between the frontal lobe and limbic system is disrupted, a child can lose control of her behavior. Damage to the temporal lobes can result in short-term memory loss that affects learning of new skills. Adults typically identify a behavior and then apply an acknowledgement or consequence to strengthen or decrease a behavior. With brain injury, if the acknowledgement center in the frontal lobe is damaged or if the connections from the limbic system to the frontal lobe become faulty, that approach may not work.

For children with brain injury, it is more important to be proactive and focus on the triggers for a behavior rather than the consequences. This can be done either by changing the environment so the trigger does not occur or, if possible, helping the child learn to recognize a trigger before

27

a crisis and find a way to diminish the effects. In addition, children with brain injury often have a low tolerance for frustration and difficulty generalizing.

Behavior is a way of communicating. This is especially true for young children, who are not able to verbally express themselves adequately. Although adults may view a behavior as inappropriate, it actually is the child's way of communicating about or adapting to his environment. Understanding the goal of the child's disruptive behavior makes it easier to change, especially if these behaviors have effectively gotten the child what he wants. Through understanding the cause of challenging behaviors, early childhood professionals can find alternative approaches in addressing these behaviors.

KEY QUESTIONS

Within most preschool settings, there are likely to be only a few
children with persistent challenging behavior. On any given day,
however, there may be a number of children who
engage in some form of disruptive behavior.
These behaviors are often related to
being in a group-care setting for
the first time, not knowing the
expectations for a setting, not
having the social skills to engage
in more appropriate behaviors,
being bored, or not knowing how to
communicate emotions in
appropriate ways.

What Is Challenging Behavior?

So, what defines challenging behavior? It is not a diagnosis and is not a condition that results in the need for a specialized education; although, it can accompany several conditions that typically do require an individualized education plan. Early childhood literature does not contain a unified and consensual definition, but the following description, from *Developing Services for People with Severe Learning Difficulties and Challenging Behaviour* by Eric Emerson et al., outlines the key features of challenging behavior: "Behaviour of such intensity, frequency, and duration that the physical safety of the person or others is likely to be placed in serious jeopardy or behaviour which is likely to seriously limit or delay access to and use of ordinary facilities."

Challenging behavior takes a number of forms, some of them low intensity and others high intensity. Most experts in the field agree that disruptive behavior has an effect on the program, the individual, the children, or the staff in the following ways:

- interferes with the child's own and/or other children's learning and development
- challenges the day-to-day functioning of the program
- challenges the right of staff and children to a safe and orderly environment
- goes beyond the normal range of what the program is able to handle, in terms of duration, frequency, intensity, or persistence
- does not respond to the usual range of interventions used by the program for inappropriate behavior

- damages the physical environment, equipment, or materials
- is inappropriate to the child's age, developmental stage, or background

From the early childhood perspective, challenging behavior is unlikely to respond to the customary strategies used in the program, regardless of the form the behavior takes. Behavior is challenging when educators' efforts fail to reduce its frequency, duration, or intensity.

DEVELOPMENTAL APPROPRIATENESS

Many behaviors regarded as challenging are simply age-appropriate; for example, a two-year-old who is not able to sit still or a five-year-old who is unable to contain her excitement and wait her turn are behaving typically for their ages. If age-appropriate behaviors become problematic, the issue lies with the adult and/or the program, not necessarily with the child.

Challenging behaviors can negatively affect the child's ability to learn and develop if not handled in an appropriate manner. These behaviors may include—but are not limited to—the following:

- tantrums
- noncompliance
- inattention
- hitting, kicking, spitting, or punching others
- refusal to share, wait, or take turns
- excluding other children
- breaking or misusing toys and equipment
- refusal to cooperate
- swearing
- shouting
- running away
- teasing or bullying

31

Other challenging behaviors may require the services of a licensed mental health professional:

- self-injury, such as head banging, self-biting, or hair pulling
- stereotyped behaviors, such as rocking, spinning, or hand flapping
- inappropriate sexual behavior, such as touching others sexually or smearing feces

ABCs of Challenging Behavior

Every instance of challenging behavior has three common components: an *antecedent, a behavior,* and a *consequence.* These are known as the ABCs of behavior.

Antecedent: an event that happens right before a behavior occurs. Antecedents, or *triggers,* can be factors in an individual's external environment, such as the clean-up routine or the beginning of group time, or internal factors, such as experiencing pain from a headache or feeling hungry.

Behavior: anything that someone does. Behaviors can be observable, such as a child riding a tricycle or shaking his head, but they can also be internal, such as feeling pain or daydreaming. Because internal behaviors can only be inferred, most behavioral interventions focus on external behaviors that are observable and measurable.

Consequence: anything that immediately happens as a result of a behavior. For example, a child may say, "juice," and the consequence of that behavior is an adult pouring the child a glass of juice. Similarly, when a young child begins to whine, the consequence may be an adult giving the child attention. Consequences can increase the likelihood of a behavior happening again, decrease the likelihood of a behavior happening again, or have no effect on the occurrence of a behavior in the future.

WHO AND WHY

Any young child, regardless of race, socioeconomic background, or culture, can exhibit challenging behavior. The young child who exhibits this behavior often will do so in response to the environment, a medical condition, socioeconomic disadvantage, or to communicate a need. Everything children do, they do for specific reasons. Throughout their lives, all children exhibit difficult or inappropriate behavior as they grow and develop. A child's underlying medical condition, age, social experiences, adverse life events, and a host of other factors can affect the type of behavior, its nature, duration, intensity, persistence, and frequency. All these aspects can be quite different in each individual.

There are many reasons why children behave in a challenging manner. Therefore, identifying those reasons can be the key to finding a solution to the problems caused by the behavior. Your analysis must include a consideration of the behavior **and the context in which it occurs.** Environmental factors may contribute to the problem. Children can react negatively to noise, heat, cold, or invasion of their space. Some children might be overly sensitive to certain stimuli, such as noise, and will react by displaying disruptive behavior.

Challenging behavior also can have an underlying medical cause, such as pain, illness, or sensory difficulties. Some forms of such behavior are particularly associated with certain conditions and disabilities. For example, repeated and involuntary body movements (tics) and uncontrollable vocal sounds can correspond with Tourette's syndrome, and ritualistic or obsessive behavior might occur in children with autism spectrum disorders.

Factors associated with socioeconomic disadvantage also influence the prevalence of challenging behavior. The poor social skills and poor language development associated with a lack of parenting skills may lead to a child exhibiting disruptive behavior. This behavior may be used as a survival mechanism in the child's environment.

Children's behavior, including challenging behavior, may be an attempt to satisfy a valid need or to express a want. Most disruptive behaviors have underlying communicative intent. Typically, the children have a need to escape or avoid a person, an activity, or a situation. Their behavior also can communicate a desire to obtain attention from someone or to gain access to activities and/or materials. In some cases, challenging behaviors may be the only way a child knows to communicate.

Challenging behaviors often serve a function. There are four main reasons they occur:
- to escape or avoid an undesirable situation (for example, avoid coming to group)
- to get positive or negative social attention (for example, receiving a hug or a redirection)
- to gain access to a desired item or activity (for example, receiving a snack or being able to go outside and play)
- to access or avoid sensory input (for example, enjoying the feeling of shaking their hands or reacting negatively to a hug)

Through a history of multiple cause-and-effect relationships, a child learns that specific behaviors can lead to specific results. For example, a child might learn that if he screams and cries at the grocery store, his parent will buy him a candy bar. A toddler might learn that every time she hits her sister, their mother will pick her up. Repeated incidents such as these reinforce the function and lead to the continued occurrence of the behaviors.

Once you understand the purpose, function, or meaning of the challenging behavior, you can begin to develop strategies to prevent it. You then can teach new skills that allow for more appropriate communication and can alter your responses (and those of their peers) to the challenging behavior.

WHEN AND WHERE

Challenging behaviors can occur at any time or in any place within the early childhood environment. Research indicates that the most likely time for disruptive behavior to occur is during transitions from one activity to another. In Chapter 5, you will find information about why routines and transitions are important for children. That chapter also provides specific strategies to help you develop and implement routines and transitions that help prevent challenging behavior from occurring in the first place.

Challenging behavior can be a result of many factors. Some children who display challenging behavior lack the communication and emotional skills to convey what they need. A child may behave in a certain way to communicate that she is experiencing physical or emotional discomfort. For example, a child may bang her head because she is in pain or may lash out because she is tired. Assessing behavior may also be part of the process to diagnose an underlying condition. For example, severe earaches or heartburn can present with aggression or self-injury in individuals who have limited communication skills.

In some conditions, a particular gene or other biological factor can affect a child's behavior or development. For example, children with conditions such as Lesch-Nyhan syndrome, Prader-Willi syndrome, Smith-Magenis syndrome, or autism may exhibit certain types of behavior more often than children without these conditions. However, not all children with a particular condition will display a particular behavior.

One of the most interesting hypotheses regarding the development of challenging behavior in children is how genes might influence behavior. The majority of researchers have realized that the interaction over a person's lifespan of the effects of genetic variation and environmental exposure is key to understanding individual differences in susceptibility to challenging behavior. Research has shown the effects of genes and environment are inextricably interwoven. On the one hand, this means that genetic influences are pervasive, though not necessarily predominant, across virtually all behaviors. On the other hand, it seems that in many (and perhaps most) instances, the effects of genes are likely to manifest through various types of interplay with the environment. Thus, some genetically influenced behaviors will affect the extent to which individuals are exposed to environmental risk. This is known as *gene-environment correlation.* For example, antisocial behavior in a parent, which is influenced by genetics, can disrupt family function and, in turn, will contribute to a child's risk of developing antisocial traits. In other words, the parent's genes are contributing to a child's risk via an environmental mechanism.

The other main way in which the effects of genes and the environment collide is through *gene-environment interaction.* Genes can influence a person's susceptibility to environmental risk. For example, stressful life events and childhood maltreatment can trigger depression in some people but not in others. There is a growing body of evidence that variation in the gene encoding of the serotonin transporter might affect the extent to which depression occurs as a consequence of exposure to adverse experiences.

Thus, genes do not "cause" behaviors or psychiatric disorders such as autism and schizophrenia. Rather, their effects on behavior are indirect and mediated by the environment. The challenge now is to more fully understand how genes and the environment interact.

COLLECTING DATA

Behavior data can serve many functions. It can be used to establish a baseline of the target behaviors to increase or decrease; compare behavior pre- and post-intervention; or be an objective means of supplying information to the child, staff, families, and administrators. Data can provide information on when and where behaviors are most likely to occur. It can describe how often, how long, how much, how intensely, with whom, and as a result of what. The analysis of data tells us whether our interventions are effective and should guide our decisions on making changes to a program, including whether to continue with an intervention. In Chapter 10, I offer information on methods of collecting data, sample graphs, and using data to create intervention plans.

Through direct observation, data can be collected on antecedents, challenging behaviors, and the consequences that follow. By analyzing the data, you can determine a potential purpose of the challenging behavior. Once a possible reason is identified, you can establish an effective intervention addressing the function of the behavior to decrease the behavior accordingly. For example, data collected on a child's tantrum behavior may reveal that the antecedent is always the teacher telling her it is time to transition to another activity, and that the consequence of this tantrum is often that she does not end up doing what she was told. This data would suggest that a possible function of the child's tantrum behavior is to escape the teacher's demands.

Long-Term Effects of Challenging Behavior on Young Children

Numerous longitudinal studies have documented both the long- and short-term effects of challenging behaviors on young children. Most of these studies conclude that serious and persistent challenging behaviors in early childhood are associated with subsequent problems in socialization, school adjustment, school success, and educational and vocational adaptation in adolescence and adulthood. When the disruptive behavior of young children is not addressed in an appropriate and timely manner, the future likelihood of poor academic outcomes, peer rejection, adult mental-health concerns, and adverse effects on their families, service providers, and communities increases.

Current research related to the development and intervention of these severe challenging behaviors suggests the following:

- Challenging behavior that appears during a child's preschool years is the single best predictor of delinquency in adolescence, school dropout, gang membership, adult incarceration, and early death.
- If challenging behavior toward others and property is not altered by the end of the third grade, it should be treated as a chronic condition, hopefully kept somewhat in check by continuing and ever-more-costly intervention.
- Children with challenging behaviors who come from families that can be characterized by coercive interactions, such as parents screaming, threatening, and imposing harsh punishment, are the most likely subgroup to grow into a life of antisocial behavior.

For the children who engage in persistent disruptive behavior and all those with whom they interact, the costs include early and persistent peer rejection, mostly punitive contacts with teachers, family-interaction patterns that all participants find to be unpleasant, predictable school failure, and lack of community integration.

Walter Gilliam of the Yale University Child Study Center conducted an extensive study into the expulsion rates of prekindergarten students across the United States. (Expulsion is the most severe disciplinary sanction that an educational program can impose on a student.) He found that prekindergarteners are expelled at a rate that is more than three times that of their older peers in grades kindergarten through 12 (6.67 percent per 1,000 preschoolers, as compared to 2.09 percent per 1,000 K–12 students). Prekindergarten expulsion rates were higher than those for K–12 students in all but three of the 40 states that fund prekindergarten.

At the classroom level, prekindergarten expulsion is not uncommon, with 10.4 percent of prekindergarten teachers expelling at least one preschooler in a given year. However, expulsion is more common in some types of centers than others: The rate of expulsion found in state-funded prekindergarten classrooms, for example, is less than one-fourth of previously reported rates from samples consisting largely of private child care centers that may not have participated in the state-funded prekindergarten system. Of the state-funded prekindergarten classrooms, teachers in school-based and Head Start centers expelled at the lowest rates. Teachers in for-profit child care and faith-affiliated centers (not state funded) expelled at rates about twice as high.

Clear differences in expulsion rates were found on the basis of child age, gender, and race/ethnicity. The highest rates of expulsion were reported for preschoolers who were on the older end of the prekindergarten age spectrum. Boys were more than four times as likely to be expelled as girls, and African-American preschoolers were about twice as likely to be expelled as Caucasian preschoolers.

The study concluded that although the benefits of high-quality early childhood education have been well documented, the positive effects of preschool are likely quite small for those children who are unable to participate because of their own disruptive behaviors. Many children may be unready for kindergarten because of difficulties regulating their emotions and behavior, forming friendships, and following adult directives. For these children, a high-quality school readiness experience is essential to starting kindergarten with the skills they need to succeed in school.

3

THE EARLY CHILDHOOD PROFESSIONAL'S MINDSET

Stanford University psychology professor Carol Dweck outlines the notion of mindset and how it can affect development and behavior in her book *Mindset: The New Psychology of Success.* Dweck asserts that everyone has one of two basic mindsets, fixed or growth.

A person with a fixed mindset believes that her talents and abilities are set in stone—either she has them or she does not. People with a fixed mindset are driven to prove themselves repeatedly, trying to look successful at all costs. Dweck has shown that when people adopt the fixed mindset, it can limit their success.

They become overly concerned with proving their talents and abilities, hiding deficiencies, and reacting defensively to mistakes or setbacks, because deficiencies and mistakes imply a permanent lack of talent or ability. People in this mindset will pass up important opportunities to learn and grow if there is a risk of unmasking weaknesses. This mindset actually leads to stagnation and declining performance.

Conversely, a person with a growth mindset knows that her talents and abilities are built over time, so she seizes opportunities for growth and success. In the growth mindset, people believe their talents and abilities can be developed through passion, education, and persistence. For them, it is not about looking smart or grooming their image. It is about a commitment to learning—taking informed risks and learning from the results, surrounding themselves with people who will challenge them to grow, looking frankly at their deficiencies, and seeking to remedy them. Building and maintaining excellent skills in the face of constant change requires a growth mindset.

Dweck shows how the growth mindset develops in childhood and early adulthood and drives every aspect of our lives, from teaching to relationships. Much of her work is based on the science of brain plasticity, the brain's ability to change as a result of experience and to be capable of learning until we die. The brain continues to create new neural pathways and alter existing ones to adapt to new experiences, learn new information, and create new memories. She describes how creative geniuses in all fields apply their growth mindsets to achieve results. Most importantly, however, Dweck demonstrates how we can change our mindset at any age.

The Importance of Mindset

In her latest book, *Mindset: How You Can Fulfil Your Potential,* Dweck's research indicates that the educator's mindset has significant effects on his behavior and performance, particularly in the face of challenging behavior. She illustrates how educators with growth mindsets are better equipped to handle such behaviors. Because they believe they can learn, change, and develop needed skills, they know that effort, hard work, and persistence can help them prevent behavioral concerns with children and intervene when they occur.

Research into such issues has led to a growing awareness of the importance of encouraging effort and persistence throughout childhood. The good news is that, in addition to deepening the understanding of effort and persistence in children, research also suggests ways teachers and other adults in children's lives can help them sustain the belief that trying to get better at something is worth it.

To develop positive behaviors, children need the support of an adult with a growth mindset who believes they can learn and develop prosocial behaviors. Without this growth mindset, adults are setting the child up for failure by believing the challenging behaviors are fixed and will not change, regardless of what the adult does. Further, people with a fixed mindset, when facing disruptive behavior, likely will respond in a manner that does not promote positive behavior, such as attempting to punish the child.

CHANGING YOUR MINDSET

The great news is that people can change a fixed mindset to a growth mindset very quickly, because our brains are powerful. So don't fall into the trap of thinking it's too late to change your mindset; it is not. Adopting a growth mindset is something we can deliberately choose to do, and it ties directly to the idea of positive professional development. We can learn to think, "What can I learn from this situation or experience?" The following steps can help you shift from a fixed mindset to a growth one.

1. **Learn to recognize your fixed mindset when it takes over.**
   When your fixed mindset starts talking, learn to recognize it. It can start whispering, for instance, when you have to decide whether or not to take a challenge: *"Are you really sure you can do it? You don't have the necessary skills! And what if you fail? Just imagine how people are going to look at you then—a failure! You'd better walk away and save your dignity."*

   When someone criticizes you: *"It is not my fault! Who does she think she is, just standing there and criticizing me?"* You will most likely get angry at the person, even if she is just sharing an honest opinion. This time the fixed mindset voice can make you run away from responsibility, or you might start to feel disappointed and insecure. By learning to recognize and replace negativity with a positive perspective, you will realize that you can increase your knowledge, abilities, and efforts.

41

2. **Respond to your fixed-mindset voice.**
   Recognize that you have a choice. Talk back to your fixed-mindset voice with a growth-mindset voice when you encounter a challenge: *"I don't know if I will be able to do it right away, but it is worth the time and effort. I'm not afraid to fail, because every successful person has failed—success cannot come instantly. If I run away now, I fail by default; so, how will that save my dignity?"*

   When you are being criticized, your growth-mindset voice can say this: *"I have to remain open to all types of criticism, because I am not perfect. Other people might actually be right. I have to take responsibility for my own actions. I can learn from this situation."*

3. **Recognize that you have a choice.**
   You—and only you—decide which voice you listen to. You decide whether or not you are going to take on a challenge wholeheartedly, learn from your setbacks, and try again. You decide to heed the criticism and act on it. Practice hearing both the fixed- and growth-mindset voices, but only listen to and act on the growth mindset. See how things will start to change.

4. **Put the growth mindset into action.**
   Ignore your fixed-mindset voice while focusing in on the voice of the growth mindset. Eventually this step will come naturally, because at some point you will stop hearing your fixed voice and will proceed with a growth mindset. If you find yourself in a difficult situation, and you handle it without even noticing the fixed-mindset voice, then you have done it. Congratulations! Now you are ready to take on more complex challenges and to develop more efficiently.

Simply noticing when you are moving into a fixed mindset can be a powerful way to switch back into growth mode. Ask yourself, "What learning is available in this situation, and how can I be open to it?" You might be able to devise new and better solutions. You also will feel less stressed about dealing with these difficulties. Consciously adopting a growth mindset can create huge shifts in your awareness and approach to solutions. It feeds your sense of purpose and will have you constantly looking for learning opportunities. Even minor, daily frustrations in your life can provide chances to learn and grow. When things do not go as planned, approach the situation with a growth mindset by looking for information in the experience that can be used to refine your approach the next time.

When you adopt a growth mindset, you can make greater attempts to seek and learn from challenging behavior. It can be difficult to avoid taking the behavior personally, but try asking probing questions that help you understand the function of the behavior and what it may be communicating to you.

THE IMPORTANCE OF RESPECT

Without mutual respect, trust, and caring, real learning is unlikely to happen. There are many bases for and levels of respect:

■ **Respect means accepting and loving each child as she is and not expecting her to do things before she is ready.** Children are born with a built-in timetable and a natural drive to achieve their own milestones just when their bodies tell them the time is right. Jean Piaget taught us that when we directly teach a child something, we take away her chances of discovering it on her own, forever. Good observers know that when a child makes a new discovery, it is like magic. You can see the twinkle in her eyes. Instead of trying to teach, we educators need to find ways to create environments where children can make as many discoveries as possible.

43

■ **Respect means understanding and using information about the way our brains develop.** Studies dating back as far as ancient Greece state the importance of teaching children in ways that follow the natural development of their minds. Biological research cited by Jack Shonkoff and Deborah Phillips in *From Neurons to Neighborhoods: The Science of Early Childhood Development* confirms what the greatest educators have been saying for years: Play is the basic universal and essential way for the human body to properly develop. Play is the only place in a child's life where all the necessary ingredients exist for physical, psychological, social, moral, and intellectual abilities to develop simultaneously. Play is consistent throughout all species, all evolution, and all history, and it makes children smarter, stronger, better human beings. It is not that difficult: Children need to play!

■ **Respect means believing in children's competence and allowing them to be explorers and self-learners.** Children are born genetically wired, ready, willing, and able to learn. They begin their quest for knowledge the minute they leave the womb. They are born with the competence to do this, so early childhood educators must become cultivators of this natural instinct.

■ **Respect means giving children uninterrupted time to explore, play, solve problems, and learn from their successes and mistakes.** Children need a lot of time to discover simple things, and adults must refrain from expecting them to speed up the natural, normal process.

■ **Respect means encouraging children to discover the available choices, permitting them to make their own choices and honoring them, while knowing their choices can sometimes make things more difficult.** Children learn from all choices equally. Preschool-age children are capable of learning that some choices are better than others. This skill becomes vitally important when the teenage years arrive and adults are not around to tell them right from wrong. When choices are limited, learning is limited.

■ **Respect means finding a way to give children the materials they need to do their work and play.** Children have the right to the quality and quantity of materials they need to accomplish the learning goals they set for themselves. Teachers must use every means available to meet these needs and then give children the time to fully utilize the materials. Children deserve clean, quality, safe learning materials.

WHEN NOTHING ELSE WORKS

They need daily access to sand, water, sensory materials, blocks, music, art, science, math, literacy activities, and dramatic play.

■ **Respect means that teachers embrace and learn about cultural and physical differences and teach children to respect these differences.** Educators must find ways to make each family culture become an integral part of the early childhood education environment.

When children know that teachers care for them and believe in them, the outcomes are much higher. Being able to care for your students marks the beginning of creating an environment where the students can respond in a caring way as well. Whether their caring will be directed toward the people around them, however, depends partly on the expectations of their teachers and on the adults who guide them and serve as models for them. Teachers can have a major effect and influence on each child's life, especially for children who lack positive influences at home. It is up to the teacher to develop a strengths-based, caring attitude and environment for all children.

Developing the capacity for respect is a lifelong challenge. Our sense of self tends to be fragile. It rises and falls as we face life's challenges with varying degrees of success. How you see yourself guides the development of self-esteem, and the people in your life act as a mirror in this process. When people who are important to you give you attention and encouragement, you see positive images of yourself. At other times, your interactions with others may make you feel unattractive, incompetent, or even invisible. As with adults, children build their sense of self-respect from their interactions with others. When they feel special and valued, children grow to respect themselves. A positive sense of self allows the maturing child to respect others.

Self-respect is at the heart of respecting others. When you can identify and appreciate your strengths and accept your vulnerabilities, it is easier to truly respect the value in others.

Individuals respect people who have traits they admire. Children begin to respect things they see in the adults who are present in their lives—both good and bad. Children raised in antisocial homes may actually respect and admire antisocial acts. They aspire to be just like Mom or Dad. Children who watch hours of television and have few adult role models may begin to value persons in the media, with all of their distorted values and unrealistic traits. This becomes a trap for children. They will never be as athletic, beautiful, powerful, and popular as the false images they see on television. And, unable to meet these ideals, they may feel inadequate and unattractive.

Hopefully, through many quality experiences with attentive adults, children will see more realistic qualities to admire. Consistency, predictability, grace under pressure, humor, and kindness are among the qualities that caring and competent adults model for children. In the classroom, children see how respected adults—their teachers—solve problems and cope with challenges. If their teachers handle conflicts by listening, thinking, staying calm, and reaching thoughtful solutions, the child comes to respect these behaviors.

Children struggle with respect in two ways. One is overt noncompliance and defiance. In this case, there is a lack of respect for classmates and for the authority figure. This is almost always associated with a poor sense of self, despite the fact that these children will often brag and distort their strengths and capabilities. This bragging is merely a protective shell for a very fragile sense of self. Often, these children do not have much attention or structure when they are away from school.

The other way in which a child struggles with respect is when he begins to say, "I'm bad," "I can't do that," "I'm stupid," or "He's better than I am." Children with a poor sense of self limit their opportunities. They do not try as hard, and as a result, they may end up creating self-fulfilling prophecies. Because they do not try new things, they do not learn as quickly as others. They fall behind. This negative cycle can be very destructive for young children.

The Interaction between Temperament and Behavior

Temperament refers to biologically based individual differences in behavior tendencies. These differences occur at an early age and remain stable over time and in various situations. Individual differences in temperament can be seen in the unique predispositions children bring to the program in terms of activity level, attention span, mood, approach to new experiences, and so on.

When the characteristics of the child do not match the expectations of others, problems can arise in the child's development. Children are at greater risk of developing emotional problems because the expectations of parents, teachers, and peers do not match their temperamental tendencies. These children are often described as difficult, because those who care for them find them difficult to manage. Stan Turecki, in his book *The Difficult Child,* says the reason these children seem challenging is because there is not a good fit between the adult's temperament and the child's temperament.

In the New York Longitudinal Study started in 1956 and conducted over a six-year time span, Alexander Thomas and Stella Chess studied nine behaviors of 141 children from 85 middle- to upper-middle-class families: activity level, rhythmicity, approach or withdrawal, adaptability, threshold of responsiveness, intensity, quality of mood, distractibility, and persistence.

47

- **Activity level** refers to the child's physical energy. Is the child constantly moving, or does the child have a relaxed approach? A high-energy child may have difficulty sitting still in class; whereas, a child with low energy can tolerate a very structured environment. The former may use gross motor skills such as running and jumping more frequently. Highly active children may channel their extra energy into success in sports and may perform well in high-energy careers.

- **Rhythmicity (regularity)** refers to the level of predictability in a child's biological functions, such as waking, tiring, hunger, and bowel movements. Does the child have a routine in eating and sleeping habits, or are these events more random? For example, a child with a high regularity rating may want to eat at 2 p.m. every day; whereas, a child lower on the regularity scale may eat at sporadic times throughout the day. As adults, irregular individuals may do better with traveling than others and may be better equipped to adapt to careers with unusual working hours.

- **Approach or withdrawal (reactivity)** refers to how the child responds (whether positively or negatively) to new people or environments. Does the child approach people or things in the environment without hesitation, or does the child shy away? A bold child tends to approach things quickly, as if without thinking. A cautious child typically prefers to watch for a while before engaging in new experiences. Children who are slow to warm up tend to think before they act. They are less likely to act impulsively, especially during adolescence.

- **Adaptability** refers to how long it takes the child to adjust to change over time. Does the child adjust to the changes in her environment easily, or is the child resistant? A child who adjusts easily may be quick to settle into a new routine; whereas, a resistant child may take a long time to adjust to a new situation. A slow-to-adapt child is less likely to rush into dangerous situations and likely will be less influenced by peer pressure.

- **Threshold of responsiveness** refers to how easily a child is disturbed by changes in the environment. Is the child bothered by external stimuli such as noises, textures, or lights, or does the child seem to ignore them? A sensitive child might lose focus when a door slams; a child less sensitive to external noises will be able to maintain focus. Highly sensitive individuals are more likely to be artistic and creative.

- **Intensity** refers to the energy level of a positive or negative response. Does the child react intensely to a situation, or does the

48

child respond in a calm and quiet manner? A more intense child may jump up and down and scream with excitement. A mild-mannered child may smile or show no emotion. Intense children are more likely to have their needs met and may have depth and delight of emotion rarely experienced by others. These children may be gifted in dramatic arts. Intense children require a lot of energy and can be somewhat exhausting.

- **Quality of mood** refers to the child's general tendency toward a happy or unhappy demeanor. All children have a variety of emotions and reactions, such as cheerful and stormy, happy and unhappy. Yet, each child biologically tends to have a generally positive or negative outlook. Serious children tend to be analytical and evaluate situations carefully.
- **Distractibility** refers to the child's tendency to be sidetracked by other things going on around him. Is the child easily distracted by what is happening in the environment, or can the child concentrate despite interruptions? An easily distracted child is engaged by external events and has difficulty returning to the task at hand; whereas, a rarely distracted child stays focused and completes the task at hand. High distractibility is seen as positive when it is easy to divert a child from an undesirable behavior but is viewed as negative when it prevents the child from concentrating.
- **Persistence and attention span** refer to the length of time a child stays on a task despite frustrations. The highly persistent child is more likely to succeed in reaching goals. A child with low persistence may develop strong social skills because she realizes other people can help.

Thomas and Chess found that while all children exhibit the same behaviors at one time or another, some children were more likely to display certain behaviors. They found that about 60 percent of children fall into one of three groups:

1. **The Easy Child**—This child shows regular eating, sleeping, and elimination cycles; has a positive approach to new situations; and can accept frustration with little fuss. He adapts to change such as new food or a new program quickly. He has a good mood most of the time and smiles often. Most of the problems reported with these children result when they are placed in situations that require responses that are inconsistent with what they learn at home.

49

2. **The Difficult Child**—This child shows irregular eating, sleeping, and elimination cycles. She displays a negative response to new situations, such as frequent and loud crying or throwing tantrums when frustrated. She is slow to adapt to change and needs more time to get accustomed to new food or people. Most of the problems reported with these children center around socialization patterns and expectations of family, school, and peer groups. If pushed to become immediately involved in a situation, these children are more likely to exhibit loud refusal and some oppositional and aggressive behavior.

3. **The Slow-to-Warm-Up Child**—This child shows negative responses of mild intensity when exposed to new situations but slowly comes to accept them with repeated exposure. He has fairly regular biological routines. Problems with these children vary depending on the other characteristics they show.

By being aware of children's temperaments, adults can anticipate when problems may arise and can take steps to prevent them. Highly active, impulsive children are likely to have problems when standing in line, sitting in group for long periods of time, or transitioning from one activity to another. Shy and slow-to-warm-up children are often upset when the usual routines are changed or when there are demands for quick responses.

By recognizing how these individual differences in children's temperaments interact with the organization and routines of your program, you can anticipate and prevent or minimize many disruptions

RESILIENCE IN YOUNG CHILDREN

Traditionally, research and practice concerning mental health and outcomes for children has focused on investigating risk factors and designing interventions and services to reduce the effects of such factors. However, risk factors are not the only predictors of outcomes for children. The observation, made more than 30 years ago, that not all children succumb to the effects of risks led to the investigation of protective factors and resilience (Werner, 1984).

Defining Resilience and Social and Emotional Intelligence

Discussions of resilience typically center around risk, vulnerability, and protective factors. The complex interplay of these factors over time determines children's outcomes. In the 1984 article "Resilient Children" in *Young Children*, Emmy Werner offered the following definitions of these factors:

- **Risk:** any factor or combination of factors that increases the chance of an undesirable outcome affecting a person
- **Vulnerability:** a feature that renders a person more susceptible to a threat
- **Protective factors:** the circumstances that moderate the effects of risk
- **Resilience:** positive adaptation in the face of severe adversities

Resilience is the term used to describe a set of qualities that fosters a process of successful adaptation and transformation despite risk and adversity. Resilience research validates prior research that has clearly established the human biological imperative for growth and development that unfolds naturally in the presence of certain environmental characteristics. Everybody is born with an innate capacity for resilience, with which they are able to develop social competence, problem-solving skills, a critical consciousness, autonomy, and a sense of purpose.

With all the risks in their lives, how can we protect children from developing behavioral problems? The great news is that most children who grow up in families with many challenges do overcome the odds and manifest resilience. Protective factors, those qualities or situations that help alter or reverse expected negative outcomes, can cultivate a child's resiliency. Protective factors can be internal (within the individual) or external (involving the family, school, and community).

The presence of at least one caring person—someone who conveys an attitude of compassion, who understands that no matter how challenging the child's behavior, the child is doing the best she can with her experience—provides support for healthy development and learning. A 1989 study by Emmy Werner and Ruth Smith, spanning more than 40 years, found that among the most frequently encountered positive role models in the lives of resilient children (outside of the family circle) was a favorite teacher who was not just an instructor for academic skills but also a confidant and positive model for personal identification.

THE CONNECTION BETWEEN RESILIENCE AND SOCIAL AND EMOTIONAL INTELLIGENCE

Emotional and social intelligence are critical components in building resilience in children. The literature and research around resilience shows many common qualities that resilient people possess. A number of these specific characteristics are also referred to as protective factors and are associated with social and emotional intelligence.

Protective factors within the child involve the ability to take control, be proactive, and make decisions about what to do instead of just letting things happen. Children with strong social and emotional intelligence take responsibility for their decisions, and they engage others when needed. In addition, individuals seem to understand and accept their abilities and limitations and know when and how much to push themselves. They are goal directed and realistic about their goals; they can discriminate when to persevere and when to quit. Finally, individuals with a positive outlook have developed coping and stress-reduction strategies. One way to help children is to develop their social and emotional intelligence, which will strengthen and build their resiliency.

Social intelligence (what Howard Gardner terms *inTERpersonal* intelligence) is separate from but complementary to emotional intelligence (Gardner's *inTRApersonal* intelligence). In his book *Social Intelligence: The New Science of Human Relationships,* Daniel Goleman splits an earlier definition in two, with emotional intelligence being inwardly focused and social intelligence being outwardly focused.

Emotional intelligence is now generally defined as self-awareness and self-management: identifying, understanding, using, and managing our emotions in positive, constructive ways. It is described as a form of social intelligence that involves the ability to monitor one's own and others' feelings and emotions, to discriminate among them, and to use this information to guide one's thinking and actions.

Social intelligence is considered other-centered: social awareness, social relationships, and engaging with others in ways that are healthy for everyone involved. The main distinction between the two is that emotional intelligence deals mainly with the personal, and social intelligence deals with the interpersonal—that fascinating array of interactions with others that affects how a person feels mentally, emotionally, and even physically.

Even though there is a clear distinction between social and emotional intelligence, they are interrelated and important constructs that educators need to develop in children. The Collaborative for Academic, Social, and Emotional Learning (CASEL) is an organization devoted to establishing social and emotional learning as essential parts of education. CASEL has described competencies associated with social and emotional intelligence that need to be developed in children:

SELF-AWARENESS

Self-aware individuals are able to recognize their emotions, describe their interests and values, and accurately assess their strengths. They have a well-grounded sense of self-confidence and hope for the future.

ABILITY TO REGULATE EMOTIONS

People with emotional intelligence are able to manage stress, control impulses, and persevere in overcoming obstacles. They can set and monitor progress toward the achievement of personal and academic goals and can express their emotions appropriately in a wide range of situations.

SOCIAL AWARENESS

Individuals who have social awareness are able to take the perspective of and empathize with others and can recognize and appreciate individual and group similarities and differences. They are able to seek out and appropriately use family, school, and community resources.

GOOD RELATIONSHIP SKILLS

People with good relationship skills can establish and maintain healthy and rewarding relationships based on cooperation. They resist inappropriate social pressure; constructively prevent, manage, and resolve interpersonal conflict; and seek and provide help when needed.

RESPONSIBLE DECISION MAKING

In making decisions, these individuals consider ethical standards, safety concerns, appropriate social norms, respect for others, and the likely consequences of various courses of action. They apply these decision-making skills in academic and social situations and are motivated to contribute to the well-being of their schools and communities.

Encouraging the Development of Social and Emotional Intelligence

Because young children often spend so much time in settings outside their own homes, early childhood professionals must understand what promotes the development of social and emotional intelligence and know how to help when development is not progressing as it should.

Resilience research has shown that a sustained, healthy relationship with at least one adult and the experience of a high-quality early childhood program can make a difference. Learning more about social-emotional intelligence in young children will enable you to better serve families while enriching your relationships with young children in your program.

Early childhood professionals need to provide a safe, nurturing, predictable, and secure environment in which all children can thrive. In addition, you need to provide a positive social-emotional climate where all children have capacity to experience, regulate, and express emotions; form close, secure relationships; explore the environment; and learn.

Specifically, you can promote social-emotional intelligence in young children by being attentive, sensitive, consistent, responsive, and interactive. Since you are a role model for social and emotional development, it is important that you have social and emotional supports in place in your own life. Finally, provide a language-rich environment where young children are encouraged to identify their feelings (and those of others) with words, express their feelings, and resolve conflicts through discourse.

Specific Strategies to Promote Social and Emotional Intelligence

- Support children as they learn self-regulation.
- Encourage children to recognize feelings in themselves and others.
- Help children learn to calm themselves when they are upset.
- Encourage the development of social awareness.
- Support children as they develop friendship skills.

SELF-REGULATION

Self-regulation, often called self-control or impulse control, involves a child's capacity for controlling emotions, interacting in positive ways with others, avoiding inappropriate or aggressive actions, and becoming an autonomous learner. Since self-regulation develops gradually, early childhood professionals can help by implementing developmentally appropriate expectations for children's behavior.

Disciplining young children when they fail to sustain attention longer than a few minutes, remain seated for extended periods of time, or calm themselves quickly when frustrated does nothing to help them learn self-regulation. Instead, model self-control in your words and actions. By providing a model in how to regulate and control behaviors and emotions, you will provide valuable input for young children in controlling their own bodies and emotions.

In addition to modeling, provide many opportunities for young children to practice and experience with adults and peers within the early childhood program. Throughout the day, help young children build the capacity to put a moment between the impulse and the action. For example, if a child wants to play on the computer right now, even though there are two other children at the technology center, you can assist the child in controlling his impulse and the feelings associated with it.

By engaging in this process, the child will develop the skill of taking time to think, plan, and come up with an appropriate response to the challenge.

Use literature during story time that incorporates the theme of self-regulation. Many stories include a main character who exhibits self-control and is able to regulate his emotions

57

and impulses. Children's books help children negotiate the social and emotional terrains of childhood while supporting their development of social and emotional intelligence.

In short, teachers of young children play a vital role in helping children develop a foundation for self-regulation skills.

RECOGNIZING FEELINGS IN SELF AND OTHERS

The emotional lessons about cultivating inner strength that children learn from the adults in their lives are powerful and long lasting. When adults ignore children's feelings, children begin to believe their feelings are not important. When adults repeatedly threaten or discipline children for a display of emotion, children learn that emotions are dangerous things that need to be held inside and hidden—an invitation to later depression or rage. When adults are unable to show angry and destructive children other ways of expressing emotion and managing their feelings, children learn it is acceptable to strike out at others or have a tantrum to get what they want.

Rather than dismissing a child's feelings, early childhood professionals can make a habit of naming emotions as readily as they name objects, thereby helping children increase their feelings vocabulary. Increased awareness of our feelings and emotions, and being able to better manage them, contributes greatly to how emotionally resilient we are or can be. The manner in which we relate to others and how they relate to us affects how we feel about ourselves, just as how we feel about ourselves can affect how we relate to and interact with others.

CALMING THEMSELVES WHEN UPSET

Watching the way an adult models a certain behavior is the strongest way children learn. If adults calm down before they act—or at least talk openly to children about losing their control if they do—this strengthens a pattern in the child of first stopping and calming down, thinking about responses, and finally picking the best one and trying it.

Research indicates that relaxation methods such as deep breathing and muscle relaxation de-escalate a child's high state of arousal. These techniques change the body's physiology from a high-arousal state (as with anger) to a low-arousal state. The goal of each of these relaxation techniques is to give children methods of relaxing in day-to-day situations during which they may notice themselves becoming tense, stressed, or anxious.

■ **Deep Breathing:** A child who is stressed and nervous breathes using shallow, rapid breaths. Shallow breathing increases the level of carbon dioxide in the bloodstream. When this level increases, it causes a constriction of the blood vessels throughout the body. This, in turn, reduces oxygen to the brain, often by more than 20 percent, which can promote dizziness, feelings of tension, and headaches.

A child who learns to control his breathing can control the way he feels. When the child is calm, offer opportunities for him to practice deep breathing. When the child is at a high state of arousal, he then will have a tool to help himself feel calmer.

The procedure calls for the child to take a deep breath, hold it, and then exhale slowly. Since deep breathing may be a complex concept for young children to grasp, introduce it through play materials such as whistles, party horns, pinwheels, and bubble wands. A familiar example can help children understand the process in concrete terms:

1. Put your hands on your tummy, breathe in all the air you can, and watch your hands rise as your belly fills up like a balloon.
2. Blow out all your air, and watch your hands go down and your belly flatten, like letting the air out of the balloon.
3. Breathe in again, and then breathe out.
4. Keep breathing in and out, as much air as you can.

■ **Humor:** The sensitive use of humor develops positive relationships with children and establishes a friendly environment. Adults can use humor in difficult moments to effectively defuse tension or to distract children who are enraged. Distractors, such as humor,

59

are highly powerful mood-altering devices that stop the cycle of escalating hostile thoughts. In other words, it is hard to stay angry when you are having a pleasant time. In addition, good moods enhance children's abilities to think flexibly and with more complexity, thus making it easier to solve problems. Laughing helps children think more broadly and associate more freely, noticing relationships that may have eluded them. Recognizing complex relationships is an important skill in problem solving, helping a person foresee the consequences of a given decision.

GUIDELINES FOR USING HUMOR

- Never use it as a weapon or to chastise or correct.
- Never make a child the butt of a joke.
- Do not take yourself too seriously.

- **Facial Push-Ups:** Facial push-ups are a neurological technique that can change the disposition of a child with the wave of your hand. Every day for three weeks, have the children participate in the activity. After three weeks, you will have conditioned their brains for this response.

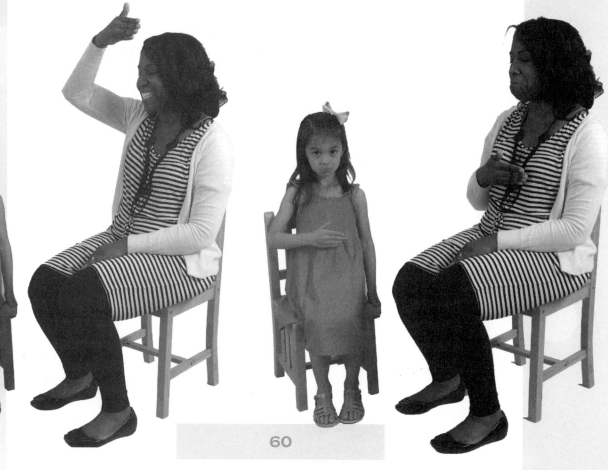

WHEN NOTHING ELSE WORKS

Model the technique and encourage the children to imitate your movements and facial expressions.

Begin by holding your hand out in front of your face. Every time your hand rises above your face, you smile. Every time you lower your hand below your chin, make a sad or angry face. Repeat the movements three or four consecutive times, always completing the activity with your and the children's hands in the up position.

After three weeks of conditioning the brain, if a child enters your classroom angry or depressed, simply wave your hand in front of the child's face and watch the student begin to smile. The brain will detect the changes in facial expression and will release positive neurotransmitters.

■ **Progressive Relaxation:** Progressive relaxation is a series of muscle-relaxing exercises that can be performed while standing, sitting, or lying down, and are extremely effective in helping a child relax certain groups of muscles. This technique works well for children who have poor impulse control because it helps strengthen the neurological pathways associated with muscle control. For each muscle group to be relaxed—the hands, arms and shoulders, shoulders and neck, eyes, jaw, face and nose, stomach, or legs and feet—use the procedure for progressive relaxation.
1. Tense the muscles to a maximum degree.
2. Notice the feelings of tension for about two seconds.
3. Relax the muscles.
4. Enjoy the feeling of relaxation for five to ten seconds.

CHAPTER 4 ■ RESILIENCE IN YOUNG CHILDREN

With children, it may be helpful to use imagery to assist them in reaching a relaxed state. Imagery, such as the following, is especially helpful for children because it attracts and maintains their interest.

- Hands: squeezing a lemon
- Arms and shoulders: stretching like a cat
- Shoulders and neck: retracting a turtle's head
- Eyes: squinting tightly to remove a foreign object
- Jaw: chewing on a jawbreaker or large piece of gum
- Face and nose: shooing off a fly
- Stomach: squeezing through a fence
- Legs and feet: standing in mud

- **Guided Imagery:** Everybody visualizes—it is a natural, largely automatic activity, like breathing or walking. Visualization refers to the conscious creation of mental sensory images for the purpose of experiencing "the inner calm."

Before you actually begin the guided visualization, you may want to have children experience inner calm. Ask the children to close their eyes for a few seconds to feel a sense of inner calm. If this activity is done regularly, it will increase children's ability to become calm on their own and will improve their attention spans and concentration. In addition, the activity will help them discover that being quiet can be meaningful, interesting, and even fun.

Some examples of guided visualizations you can use with children could include the following:

- a special place in nature, such as a lake, woods, or mountains
- a favorite trip, such as to the zoo, a park, or a children's museum
- an imaginary journey, such as to a magical land or to a faraway planet

- **Stretching:** Children can be taught the difference between muscle tension and relaxation. They need to recognize that stretching and relaxing a muscle group can make them feel better and can relieve negative tension during a task, which reinforces the use of

WHEN NOTHING ELSE WORKS

stretching for relief. Stretching should be done slowly and held for at least a six-second count to maximize the potential value. For young children, you can be creative by using not only counting but also ABCs, a rhyme, or a well-known verse to keep the children's interest while holding or completing each stretch.

■ **Affirmations:** Because of the negative criticism children may be experiencing in their lives, it is important for us to provide affirmations. Affirmations note the positive things children do and communicate attention, acceptance, and approval. Since children innately want to please their parents and teachers, one of the most powerful techniques for eliciting appropriate behavior is to comment on how well they are doing.

Affirmations assist children in developing a positive self-concept. A positive self-concept will help children have more confidence in their abilities. As children mature, these external affirmations become internalized. Affirmations help children become independent and competent. Finally, affirmations help children develop *self-efficacy,* the belief that one has mastery over the events of one's life and can meet challenges as they appear. Since affirmations help develop children's competency, they strengthen a child's self-efficacy, making a child more willing to take risks and seek out more challenging experiences. When children develop this mindset, they will be more likely to make the best use of whatever skills they have or do what it takes to develop them. There are numerous ways to incorporate affirmations into your program:

■ **Sing:** Singing can play an important role in giving recognition to children. Include songs at group time that take turns singing the name of each student and focusing briefly on that child.

■ **Provide pictures:** Put up a poster with photographs taken of all the children engaging in activities they enjoy. Put out a photograph album highlighting the events of the year and including photos of each child.

■ **Highlight interests:** Create graphs of children's interests, and post these throughout the classroom.

■ **Display artwork:** Children's artwork can be simply framed and displayed throughout the classroom.

■ **Tell stories:** Children can create and dictate their own stories that can be transcribed by an adult. These stories can be posted in the classroom.

CHAPTER 4 ■ RESILIENCE IN YOUNG CHILDREN

Another technique that may be beneficial in developing children's positive self-concepts is to write affirmations at the top or bottom of the mirrors in the classroom. Every time a child looks in the mirror, she will see herself with the affirmation. This will continually reinforce this positive concept. The following affirmations can be posted on any mirror:

- You are a helper.
- You are a friend.
- You are a neighbor.
- You are an artist.
- You are a listener.

Finally, you can have children develop affirmations based on the letters of their names. For example, if a child's name is Bill, you could have the following affirmations or positive descriptors associated with it:

Brilliant
Intelligent
Likeable
Loveable

Not only can you do a child's first name, you can also develop affirmations for the last name. This is an excellent family-engagement activity, with the family providing the affirmations associated with each letter of their child's name.

- **Music:** Music can be used as an effective relaxation strategy, especially for young children. According to Richard Edwards and Donald Hodges in "Neuromusical Research: An Overview of the Literature," in *Neurosciences in Music Pedagogy*, music brings about many positive physical changes within the human body:
    - **Brain waves:** Music with a strong beat can stimulate brain waves to resonate in sync with the beat, with faster beats bringing

sharper concentration and more alert thinking, and a slower tempo promoting a calm and relaxed state (see Table 4.1). In addition, the change in brain-wave activity levels can also enable the brain to shift speeds more easily on its own as needed, which means that music can bring lasting benefits to a child's state of mind, even after she has stopped listening.

■ **Breathing and heart rate:** With alterations in brain waves come changes in other bodily functions. Those governed by the autonomic nervous system, such as breathing and heart rate, can also be altered by the changes music can bring. This can mean slower breathing, slower heart rate, and an activation of the relaxation response. This is why music can help counteract or prevent some of the damaging effects of chronic stress, greatly prompting relaxation.

■ **State of mind:** Music can also be used to bring about a more positive state of mind, helping to keep anxiety at bay. This can help prevent the stress response from wreaking havoc on the body and can help keep creativity and optimism levels higher.

■ **Overall positive benefits:** Music can lower blood pressure, boost immunity, ease muscle tension, and more.

With so many benefits and such profound physical effects, it is no surprise that so many view music as an important tool to help the body and mind stay healthy.

TABLE 4.1

MUSIC TEMPO AND ASSOCIATED USES

Beats per Minute	Recommended Usage
45–50	Imagery, physical/mental relaxation, concentration, and thinking. This is great for study, testing, work groups, and computer time.
55–70	Effective for learning new material, writing in journals, and thinking creatively.
70–80	Group work, moderate activity, inspiration for creative group work.
80–130	Use for motivation and productivity. Great for task completion and kinesthetic activities. Seldom effective otherwise at break time or to call back a group from break.

Music can be a powerful tool in relieving stress and can be used in several ways. Listed below are some musical albums to use for relaxation and stress relief:

Best of Silk Road by Kitaro—This is a great mix of soothing but energizing music that is perfect for stress relief.

In My Time by Yanni—For soothing tension, this is one of the best albums. The songs are beautifully played on the piano with orchestral backup, no vocals. They have a calming, contemplative, uplifting quality that is great for stress reduction.

Vivaldi: The Four Seasons—Antonio Vivaldi's violin concertos promote a calming atmosphere any time of the day.

A Day without Rain by Enya—Her beautiful, ethereal voice over the gentle orchestration makes Enya a favorite for stress reduction. The calm pace of the music is perfect for someone who wants soothing music for more active listening rather than mere ambiance.

The Pachelbel Canon with Ocean Sounds by Anastasi—You may not know Johann Pachelbel's "Canon in D" by name, but you almost certainly have heard it! His melody adds magic to wedding-ring commercials everywhere and is the epitome of soothing classical music. This album has the sounds of ocean surf mixed in, which is perfect for guided visualization.

Social Awareness

In today's society, individuals often have limited social awareness, including *empathy*—the ability to understand and share the feelings of others. Digital communication, social networking, video conferencing, and other forms of new media contribute to this loss of empathy. After all, it is much easier to say something negative about others if you do not have to say it to their faces. And if someone does not feel like engaging in your problems, he can simply log off or even "unfriend" you. Distance is an easy option.

The trouble is that when there is no empathy, when we do not work to understand the needs of others, there is also a significant loss of trust. If individuals do not really know what you are thinking and feeling, they trust you less and isolate themselves more. This can have major implications for education where trust is essential for development and learning.

When you respond to the needs, values, and feelings of other people, you gain their trust. Social awareness helps young children understand and function in the world in which they live. During their early years, children are developing their values and attitudes about themselves, other children, their families, their community, and the world. Young children in particular can require considerable help in learning how to relate to other people and how to behave positively and appropriately in social situations. Offer children a broad range of experiences and expose them to a variety of people and materials, without gender, racial, ability, or cultural biases.

Young children gradually develop their ability to show social awareness through empathy, compassion, and caring. The most powerful way to encourage social awareness in children is to first ensure that children are nurtured and well cared for themselves. Then, let them see adults modeling empathy, compassion, and caring.

For infants, the concepts of giving and getting begin at birth. The development of empathy and emotional and social intelligence originate in the first months and years of life. Infants often respond to the cries of other infants by crying themselves. Happy infants will change their expressions of joy to looking away or crying when their caregiver looks sad or talks in a depressed tone.

As the child enters toddlerhood, he must work through the challenges of discovering what's "mine" and the need to share and give to others. Toddlers' empathetic responses may be what they themselves would like to have happen in a similar situation. For example, a toddler who sees a friend fall and get hurt may take his own mother over to the hurt child, even though the hurt child's mother is also present. Children learn about giving from adults who value sharing, caring, and helping others and who model generosity and encourage children's opportunities to experience caring and helping.

67

Preschool children become able to recognize and name emotions, particularly happiness, sadness, anger, surprise, and fear. They also realize that another child can feel differently from how they feel. Preschool children often look at adults for facial expressions and listen for their tones in new situations to determine what action to take. Comforting a friend in distress (for example, offering a blanket to a crying child or patting his back) is often seen in preschoolers, especially those who have seen these behaviors modeled by adults.

Preschoolers tend to believe in absolutes (right or wrong with no grey areas). Although they still tend to be primarily egocentric and think that others see things the same way they do, they are beginning to move toward seeing the perspectives of others. Sharing is becoming easier for most preschoolers.

Three- to five-year-olds often use role playing to act out and learn more about feelings and roles. Preschool children also respond to guidance, through dramatic play or real-life situations, in how to help others. For example, a teacher may suggest, "Your baby doll is crying. Maybe if you gently rock her and hold her close, she will feel better."

Some—perhaps many—early childhood educators would say that promoting social awareness is one of the fundamental missions of early childhood programs today, and that it needs to be woven into many of the daily activities. Establish a caring community by consistently implementing group activities such as classroom meetings, by dealing with disagreements and conflicts in class in an open way, by encouraging cooperative learning activities, and by reading books that focus on social issues familiar to the children themselves.

WHEN NOTHING ELSE WORKS

DEVELOPING RELATIONSHIPS

Relationships enable young children to care about people by establishing the human connection between self and others. As a consequence of early relationships, young children learn friendship skills by seeking to understand the feelings, thoughts, and expectations of others, as well as grasping the importance of cooperation and sharing.

The young child's identity is shaped by the interactions she has with others who are significant in her life—parents, childcare providers, and other family members. The National Scientific Council on the Developing Child asserts that the quality of these early relationships has a far more significant influence on early learning than previously understood.

THE EARLY CHILDHOOD ENVIRONMENT

Young children learn best in an environment where they feel safe to explore, experience, and interact. The environment tells them how to act and respond; for example, a large, open space in the center of the classroom clearly invites young children to run across the area. Keeping things simple sparks creativity: The fewer materials available for use, the more children will use their imaginations to create interesting activities–activities that can include conflict. The arrangement and materials in the environment will determine the areas where children focus their work and will influence the number of conflicts that occur or the way the group works together. An effectively designed classroom can positively influence all areas of young children's development, especially social and emotional skills such as cooperation and persistence.

Early childhood classrooms have four variables that contribute to instability: unpredictability, multidimensionality, simultaneity, and immediacy.

- **Unpredictability**—Mitigate this aspect of the classroom environment by using routines and transitions.
- **Multidimensionality**—Acknowledge the realties of daily life and link them to learning.
- **Simultaneity**—Many events occur in an early childhood classroom at the same time. Quicklly decide which events require immediate attention and which can wait to be addressed or selectively ignored.
- **Immediacy**—Learn to address young children quickly because they are just beginning to develop self-regulation.

These variables underscore the need for classrooms to be stable, predictable, and nurturing.

Consider the following adaptations as you design your classroom environment:

- **Aesthetics:** The design of the physical environment powerfully affects all aspects of an early childhood program. Purposeful and engaging environments blend and balance the best elements of home, school, and community life and help the children feel welcome and respected. Create a warm and inviting environment filled with endless possibilities for inventing and creating. At the end of the day, the children will not feel depleted; on the contrary, they will feel excited about what the next day will bring.

  Create an aesthetically pleasing environment enriched and equipped with materials from home, nature, and from the children and adults themselves. When developing this type of environment, take into account how the immediate surroundings can awaken a young child's senses; for example, use soothing aromas, provide a variety of different textures to feel, offer calming sounds, and include visuals and objects that are pleasing to the eye.

- **Softness:** Young children who spend most of their day in one environment need surfaces that respond to them, not hard surfaces that they must conform to. Rugs, couches, pillows, and the lap of a caregiver all respond to a child's basic physical needs. Beanbag chairs are an excellent alternative for young children who have difficulty remaining in an assigned location for an extended period of time. When the child sits in the beanbag chair, the chair automatically conforms to the child's body contours. This forces the child to exert energy to exit the chair. In addition, the beans in the chair gently massage the skin, creating a calming effect.

■ **Personal space:** Young children need the opportunity to have personal space to develop a sense of who they are, so provide each child with a space that she can call her own. This will help young children learn about caring for their possessions, which helps them develop a sense of autonomy. In addition, understanding what is theirs is the first stage of developing an understanding of the concept of sharing. Define the children's personal spaces with cubbies, baskets, or plastic containers, and encourage the children to respect personal-space boundaries and the important items contained within them.

■ **Visual cueing:** Advances in the neurosciences have provided information on how individuals process sensory information. This research has indicated that individuals process 75 percent of information visually. When the brain develops, it does so from back to front. The primary responsibility of the occipital lobe, located in the back of the brain, is to process visual information. This lobe is fully developed by the age of one, indicating that young children's ability to process visual information far exceeds any of the other senses. Secondly, when visual stimuli enter through the eyes, they need to travel through the entire brain to reach the occipital lobe. About 75 percent of neurons connect directly to the visual information as it travels through the brain, essentially overriding every other sense.

Young children from dysfunctional home environments typically learn to cope by tuning out noise and negative comments. Unfortunately, this also means that they can also tune out important auditory cues. To assist these children in developing to their full potential, it is vital to incorporate visual cues into the classroom.

How to Organize and Structure the Environment to Help Every Child Succeed

Discovering how to turn environmental challenges into learning opportunities takes time and persistence. Develop an action plan and make choices about how to best use your resources. Set the stage by creating a child-centered environment that is based on developmentally appropriate activities, expectations, and techniques and is organized to address positive discipline. Use a preventative approach: intentionally develop the children's self-esteem, provide clear communication and appropriate interactions with adults and peers, and implement systematic interventions when necessary.

Children manage on their own when the environment is well-organized, with open pathways that clearly lead to activities that offer enough to do. They can move freely from one activity to another, giving the teacher an opportunity to attend to individual children according to their needs. Conversely, an environment that is not well-organized creates problem areas, such as dead spaces that encourage wandering and unruly behavior, and pathways that lead nowhere or interfere with play already in progress. In a poorly organized environment, children depend on the teacher for guidance; therefore, the teacher's behavior becomes directive. When teachers spend a great deal of time directing group behavior, they have less time to assist individual children, who in turn have fewer opportunities to participate in free play.

Consider the structure of the room: location, furniture, storage and display, and boundaries. Locate related activities near each other and convenient to the contours and restrictions of the room. For example, do not put the quiet area near the sink or put the block corner just inside the front door. Instead, consider placing the book exploration area next to the quiet area. The block center will work well placed near the dramatic play space or the music area. Create pathways that children can use to move between centers. The overall layout should be a maze, a path that leads a child deliberately from one activity to another. Keep these pathways at least three feet wide to maintain easy and safe access throughout the room for all members of the classroom community.

Even environments that are carefully designed and equipped

for young children may not meet the needs of children with disabilities.

Consider the adaptations needed for any child with special needs,

whether those needs are physical challenges, learning concerns,

or social and emotional issues. Make all members

of the classroom community feel welcome and supported,

and follow accessibility guidelines.

Consider furniture placement carefully. You can prevent many disruptive behaviors by establishing clear boundaries for the activity centers. Boundaries such as a solid half-wall, a shelf, or a carpet line or strip of masking tape on the floor indicate to a child where to go and when to stop. Use shelves as solid boundaries to protect floor-based activities, such as the block area. Use more fluid boundaries, such as a canopy, a change in wall color, or a large area rug, to delineate the quiet area, the book area, and so on.

75

Young children love to sit on the floor because there they have more control of their bodies and can adjust their height according to the activity. Place tables of varying heights for the children to use as work surfaces. Sometimes using a table and chairs can be limiting; however, tables can be adjusted to standing height, so a child would not have to bother with the chair. A table 8–12 inches high would enable a child to kneel and easily access the engagement area. One creative teacher in a preschool classroom sawed off the legs of the table so it stood a foot above the ground. This table became the centerpiece of the writing center, which then became the most popular area in the classroom. If chairs are necessary in a particular center, make sure that the children's feet can touch the floor.

Provide easily accessible storage and display center materials. Organized, accessible materials promote independence, encourage the educational process by prolonging concentration, inhibit distraction, and encourage child-initiated discovery. Fewer pieces will be lost, the number of physical conflicts will be lessened, and the frustrations of waiting will be minimized. Place shelves at right angles to the walls, so that valuable wall space can be used to showcase children's work. Instead of cramming books into a bookshelf, spread them out on a display to make them more inviting for young children.

Clutter can make or break the mood of an environment. Jumbled toys, naked dolls, missing puzzle pieces, and unclaimed clothing will make a room chaotic and uninviting. Consider using two shelves in each activity area with a limited variety of toys in organized containers. Rotate the

WHEN NOTHING ELSE WORKS

materials frequently to keep interest high. This method is much more likely to encourage an industrious and harmonious setting.

Reflect the importance of children in the environment by including examples of their works-in-progress, finished products, and images of the children themselves. Communicate belonging by letting every child in the program see his work and photos of himself and his family throughout the building, not just in the classroom. Change displays of children's work routinely to reflect their current activities and explorations.

Display pictures of all kinds of families, including single-parent, grandparent, interracial, multiethnic, same-gender, and adoptive families. Use the entire center to reflect diversity—race, ethnicity, languages, gender roles, traditions, and customs—through artwork, photos, posters, signs on the wall, books, and dolls. In the classroom, post parent boards, newsletters, and announcements, and provide a variety of diverse materials such as puzzles, magazines, people sets, activity books, music, art materials, fabrics, costumes, and artifacts.

77

USE THE ENVIRONMENT TO PREVENT CHALLENGING BEHAVIOR

When designing your early childhood environment to prevent challenging behaviors from occurring, consider five ideas:

1. **Group-time areas:** This area needs to be large enough for the entire group to meet together while sitting comfortably without being crowded.

2. **Location of centers:** Divide the room into several distinct interest centers, placing quiet centers near each other and noisier centers where they will not disturb the quiet areas.

3. **Shapes and boundaries of centers:** Provide well-defined boundaries consisting of low shelves, screens, furniture, and so on. Place furniture in a way that clearly indicates its use; for example, two places at an easel communicates how many children may work at a time. Section off tables with masking tape or contact paper over construction paper strips; use carpet squares to define working or sitting spaces. A Hula-Hoop can be a moveable boundary for an individual activity.

4. **Accessibility of materials:** Display materials neatly, making sure that the children can get their materials without assistance. Be sure that the children know clearly what they may use and what does not belong to them.

5. **Orderly organization and use of materials:** Labeling shelves and work areas solves many classroom clean-up problems. Cut small pictures from catalogs or draw simple illustrations to use as material labels. Mount the images on 3"x 5" cards, and write the names of classroom items under the images. These labels can be used to show children where specific items belong. Use area signs to help children associate specific behaviors, activities, and materials with a particular space. Visual cues, such as procedure cards, footprints to designate numbers of children at a center or how to line up, and directional arrows for traffic patterns, help children learn to use the environment in an orderly manner.

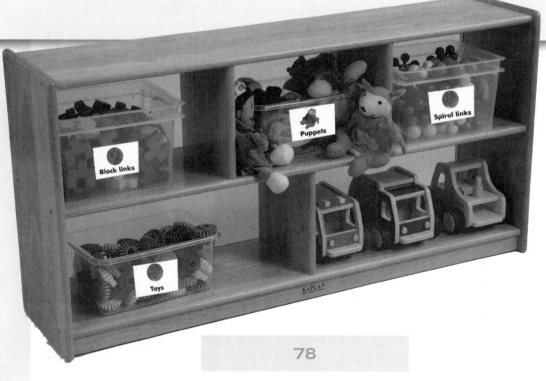

ROUTINES AND TRANSITIONS

Once you have an organized structure in place, you will need to add the next layer—creating a calm, predictable classroom atmosphere. Through establishing a clear routine and easing transitions and by setting clear, reasonable, age-appropriate expectations, you can set a positive tone in the classroom community and avert many challenging behaviors.

Routines and transitions compose much of a child's day. They can help preschoolers gain a sense of self and community and can build important self-regulation abilities. When the children know what to expect, routines and transitions also help reduce the children's uncertainty and anxiety. They provide children with predictability and stability in their immediate environment. Not only are routines important for young children, they are equally important to early childhood educators. Routines and transitions reduce the complexity of planning and give more opportunities to focus on the preschoolers. If routines and transitions are not established in the beginning of the year, early childhood educators will spend a significant amount of their planning time developing routines for activities and managing transitions.

Young children thrive in a well-ordered and predictable environment where arrivals and departures, mealtimes, nap times, and toileting are dealt with consistently. Daily routines offer young children a sense of stability and a feeling of warmth and caring from their teachers. The challenge is to develop appropriate daily routines that offer children a sense of consistency and security yet remain flexible and responsive to the individual needs of each child. The National Association for the Education of Young Children (NAEYC) emphasizes the importance of predictable, structured daily routines in which children feel secure and teachers seek opportunities to expand on children's ideas and interests.

Routines typically follow the same sequence and have a set beginning, middle, and end. The beginning of a routine should include cues about the event or activity that is about to occur. Choosing one cue that is specific to each routine can help young children prepare themselves

CHAPTER 5 ■ THE EARLY CHILDHOOD ENVIRONMENT

for what comes next and recall that sequence when the event reoccurs. The cue should be presented at the start of a routine to initiate student action. The middle of a routine includes all the steps needed to complete the task. The difficulty of the routine should be appropriate for the ages and abilities of the children in the group. Some young children might be able to complete each step independently, but others may need partial physical assistance or intermittent direction. The end of a routine indicates to young children that the activity or event is now finished.

Transitions—the process of moving from one activity to another—are often difficult for young children. Through transition activities that prepare and prompt children for changes, classrooms can be calm and organized with happy, cooperative children. Transition times, when used properly, can become teachable moments.

The Division for Early Childhood (DEC) of the Council for Exceptional Children emphasizes that transitions should be structured to promote interaction, communication, and learning. Disruptive behavior is more likely to occur when there are too many transitions, when all the children transition at the same time in the same way, when transitions are too long and young children spend too much time waiting with nothing to do, or when clear instructions are not given.

Preschoolers may engage in challenging behavior when they do not understand the expectations for the transition or when a staff member or substitute teacher implements transitions differently from the regular classroom teacher. Some preschoolers have a difficult time with transitions because of disabilities or limited communication, social-emotional, or cognitive skills. For example, a child with a developmental delay or hearing loss may take longer to process directions. If adults give too many instructions at once or give oral directions without cues, the child may be confused. Additionally, a young child may engage in challenging behavior because she does not want to stop what she is doing or does not want to go to the next activity, or because the transition occurs without warning.

Plan routines and transitions carefully, and practice them with the children, especially early on in the program. Make sure the children know when those routines and transitions will take place, and give them as much assistance as you can to help them recognize transitions and the importance of routines. Is it worth the time and effort? Absolutely.

As you reflect on the transitions and routines within your program, there are a number of crucial points to consider:

1. Minimize the number of transitions as much as possible. While transitions must occur, young children benefit from a schedule that limits the need to switch too frequently. Too many transitions results in stress for both children and adults.

2. Plan ahead. Long before children arrive, reflect on major transitions determined by the schedule, and develop plans. During the planning, look first at the classroom environment to make sure it supports what is expected during the transition. Determine creative ways of using staff to build flexibility into transitions. Be fully prepared for the day so you can focus on encouraging young children during transitions. And, don't forget that an element of fun can promote a successful transition.

3. Teach children what is expected to help them develop self-regulation skills. During well-planned transitions, children anticipate and take the lead in doing what is needed to move to the next activity. You support self-management by actively teaching the sequence of activities— what comes first, second, and so on.

Effective teaching allows you to engage children, moving beyond giving orders or needing to constantly tell children what to do next, and enables you to focus on children who might truly need it.

Constantly evaluate the effectiveness of transition plans and adjust as needed. Remember to be flexible and implement new strategies as you evaluate the transitions. Whenever a transition is necessary, allow enough time for the children to participate at their own pace. If a transition is too long, change it.

There are a number of strategies that support smooth transitions between activities and encourage children as they learn these transitions:

■   Offer verbal cues, such as, "Five minutes before group time."
■   Pair children with peers who can model behavior and assist with difficult transitions.
■   Permit children to transition from one area to another when they are ready, to avoid having them wait for the entire group, which could result in challenging behavior. If the children must wait, consider having a number of manipulatives ready that the children can engage with until everyone is ready to transition to the next activity.

- Acknowledge a child after the transition: "Carlos, you cleaned up the dramatic play area and walked over to the carpet to get ready for group time."

In many instances, early childhood professionals might raise their voices or shout to obtain children's attention. When the adults raise their voices in most cases, children will ignore the directive. Use an established visual signal or an auditory signal other than the human voice to indicate that it is time to stop, look, and listen. These strategies are referred to as *boomerang signals* or *attention signals* that help children stop, look at the adult, and listen for what comes next. Choose a signal the children have to watch for, such as two fingers held in the air or a "high five" sign, or something they must listen for, such as a hand clap, a strike on a triangle, or two taps on a drum. With most children, either option works well. With more challenging groups of children, you will probably find an audible signal to be more effective than a visual one. Whatever the signal, it is reasonable to expect the children to stop, look, and listen within four seconds of seeing or hearing it.

You may need to provide support for some young children who have difficulty following the established transitions. For example, some children with auditory processing and receptive language concerns may need photos to help them anticipate what activity is next. Other children who have a hearing impairment or who are English-language learners might need directions given in sign language or in their native language. Some preschoolers need an individual alert to let them know that soon it will be time to transition to a new activity.

Even though all routines and transitions are important, two deserve special attention: arrival and departure. They will set the tone for the day and help children develop a positive mindset toward their early childhood experience.

It is important for the teacher to meet and greet the

WHEN NOTHING ELSE WORKS

preschoolers as they arrive. Greeting the child as she enters the room sends a message that she is welcome in the environment and sets a positive tone for the rest of the day. Also, her response provides the teacher with insight about her disposition and emotional state.

Let the children know what is expected upon entering the classroom, such as washing hands or putting coats away. Departure should follow a set routine as well, such as evaluating the day's activities, distributing children's work or notices to families, and asking the children to put on their coats. Be sure to individually acknowledge the departure of each child. It lets him know that you value him as part of the group and gives you the opportunity to celebrate his achievements during the day.

Following is a simple checklist to help you assess the effectiveness of transitions:

1. Think through the steps of a routine.
2. Introduce the routine in small groups by using the daily schedule to clarify when the routine takes place.
3. Develop procedure cards that contain pictures of each step of the activity.
4. Point to each pictured step while giving simple directions.
5. Demonstrate each step yourself, making sure you point out the space and materials used.
6. Capitalize on the power of humor to add emphasis and to avoid potential problems.
7. Select volunteers to go through the routine or use peer models to demonstrate the appropriate behavior.

DEVELOPMENTALLY APPROPRIATE EXPECTATIONS FOR YOUNG CHILDREN

When you stop to think about it, we actually have quite a few specific expectations of young children. Too often, these desired behaviors or outcomes are assumed on our part and never explained to the children. It is much easier for children to meet a teacher's expectations when they know what those expectations are. Communicate expectations by directly teaching the children what to do, providing opportunities for the children to practice what is expected of them, and consistently responding to children's behavior. When developing expectations for the program, there are some key points to consider:

- Expectations must be clear, concise, and explicit. Children must understand what to do and know how to behave.
- Expectations must be reasonable, positively worded, and relatively few in number. Most young children can reasonably remember three to five of them.
- Expectations must be taught systematically and in context, so children can learn why the behaviors are important and how to engage in them.

Research in the areas of Positive Behavior Support and Pyramids of Intervention has demonstrated that establishing and teaching expectations in the early childhood environment has a positive effect on the classroom climate and prevents challenging behavior from occurring.

EXAMPLES OF POSSIBLE EXPECTATIONS IN AN EARLY CHILDHOOD AND KINDERGARTEN ENVIRONMENT:

- Be safe.
- Walk, do not run, inside the building.
- Keep feet on the ground.
- Keep hands and body to yourself.
- Be respectful.
- Use an "inside voice" when in the building.
- Speak kindly to others.
- Be responsible.
- Take care of equipment and materials.
- Clean up after yourself.
- Be a team player.
- Share.
- Take turns.
- Include everyone.

In his book *Teaching,* Jere Brophy presents a synthesis of the principles of effective teaching that have emerged from research in classrooms:

- Teachers who establish and maintain norms for an effective learning environment spend more time teaching because less time is usurped by discipline.
- Norms that engender a supportive learning environment include acting and interacting responsibly, treating others with respect and concern, and fostering a learning orientation.
- Effective school-wide norms can be established through a school-based program that focuses on supportive interactions among children.

When teachers follow these steps to establish, teach, and enforce classroom guidelines and expectations, they can anticipate increased rates of compliance, fewer office referrals for guideline violations, more academic engaged time, and greater personal satisfaction with regard to classroom management of instruction.

TEACHING DEVELOPMENTALLY APPROPRIATE EXPECTATIONS

At the beginning of the school year, explain, teach, and acknowledge what is expected of the children while in the classroom. Is it possible to do all this on the first day? Absolutely not. Humans can process only a finite amount of information in a given time. Instead, prioritize the expectations and discuss the most important ones on the first day. Then, throughout the first several weeks, continue to teach, model, discuss, and acknowledge what is expected of the children.

Once the expectations have been developed, they can be used to address specific concerns in other areas of the program. Table 5.1 is an example of a matrix of expectations and guidelines developed to address specific locations.

Table 5.1

MATRIX OF EXPECTATIONS

Expectation	Classroom	Playground	Hallways
Be respectful.	Use a gentle touch.	Take turns.	Use a gentle touch.
Be safe.	Walk inside.	Sit on bikes, slides, and swings.	Walk inside.
Be a team player.	Share.	Include everyone.	Stay together.
Be responsible.	Use materials as intended.	Slide down the slide.	Watch where you are walking.

If a child is exhibiting challenging behavior, determine if the child understands the expectations and guidelines associated with that situation. There are a number of strategies adults can use to teach children what is expected in the program:

■ **Model:** Both adults and children can be models for their peers. For example, two young children can demonstrate taking turns while the adult provides a script focusing on that expectation. For children to fully understand an expectation, they will need to hear it explained or see it modeled multiple times in various ways.

- **Cue:** Visual cues, such as photographs, clip art, or symbols, can assist children in understanding expectations and knowing what to do. Teachers can place some visual cues next to the guidelines, so the children receive immediate visual feedback of what is expected. Strategically place visual cues throughout the classroom; for example, laminated pictures on the floor cue children about where to line up, and a picture of students in line placed on the door frame provides children with immediate feedback on how to line up. During group time, the teacher can feature a picture of a child sitting quietly. Guidelines for listening, including a visual symbol to represent what is expected, can be located next to the picture of each expectation; for example:

  1. Eyes Looking Forward
  2. Ears Opened
  3. Mouth Closed
  4. Hands in Lap
  5. Feet Crossed
  6. Bottom on Floor

  A paper strip with photos of the clean-up routine reminds children what to do after breakfast, lunch, or snack time. In addition to verbally discussing of any changes in the daily schedule, a picture of an event or person on the daily calendar can cue children that something different is happening that day or that someone such as a prospective family or an intervention specialist will be visiting the program.

One of the most challenging activities for both teachers and children is cleaning up at the conclusion of free-play or free-choice time. To help children remember what to do at clean-up time, provide a picture of what the center looks like before children begin to interact with the materials there. The photo will serve as a visual cue of what is expected and as a guideline for putting materials away.

WHEN NOTHING ELSE WORKS

- **Practice:** Promote children's development of self-regulation by creating opportunities to practice the expectations associated with certain challenging behavior. Children can follow the expectations, including the specific guidelines that have been established and monitored by someone else, usually the teacher. As they learn, children can apply the guidelines to themselves; for example, if a child wants to play at the sensory table, he will need to put on a smock. Children can develop their own guidelines for each other and monitor how these guidelines are implemented. For example, in the dramatic play area, children might establish guidelines about taking turns holding the baby dolls and might make sure nobody breaks those guidelines.

There are a number of different techniques for teaching and acknowledging the expectations that have been established in a program:

- **Expectations on a ribbon:** Obtain a spool of ribbon that is at least a half-inch wide. Cut the ribbon into strips about 9-12 incheslong. With a marker, write one of the expectations of the program on the strip. Review with the child what has been written on the ribbon, then tie the ribbon onto the child's book bag. In most instances, when the child returns home, a family member will ask why the ribbon is there. This provides an excellent opportunity to reinforce the expectation that had been established in the classroom and generalize it to another environment such as the child's home. The process can be repeated with a different expectation every week. The expectation ribbons usually remain on the book bag, and each time the child sees them, they automatically reinforce the expectations that have been established in the program.

- **Expectation books:** Since most programs have digital cameras and color printers, the expectations book is easy to develop. With the children, decide which expectation is the primary focus of the book. For example, the expectation might be being safe and using gentle hands. Take pictures of the children using their gentle hands, and develop a caption to accompany each photograph, such as the following:

- We use our gentle hands to pet the gerbil.
- We use our gentle hands to greet another child.
- We use our gentle hands to help a child put away the blocks.
- We use our gentle hands to play with other children.

Add the captions to the photographs of children modeling the behavior, then bind the pages together with a title on the cover, such as *Being Safe—We Use Our Gentle Hands in the Classroom, on the Playground, and in the Hallways.* Consider using the expectation books as a family-involvement activity. Let each child take the book home and either have a family member read the book to her or have the child work on reading the book to a family member.

We use our gentle hands to play with other children.

In addition, expectation books can be used as an intervention strategy for a specific child who needs additional support in following the expectation within the classroom. For example, if a child climbs on equipment and runs in the classroom and hallways instead of walking, create an expectation book focusing on being safe. Feature photographs of that particular student modeling the expectation of being safe in situations such as walking in the classroom and hallways and keeping feet on the ground.

Expectation books are also a wonderful intervention strategy to address the challenging behavior of bullying. Bullying is defined as aggressive behavior usually repeated over time that involves an imbalance of power or strength. One example of bullying behavior exhibited in early childhood programs is exclusion. Since bullying behavior is in direct conflict with the expectation of being a team player, an expectation book displaying a variety of examples of being a team player could be developed. The book would specifically focus on including everyone in activities, especially during unstructured games that children initiate with others.

WHEN NOTHING ELSE WORKS

■ **Music:** For children, music is part of daily life. Most children enjoy music and respond positively and instinctively to it. Music can also enhance learning and development in areas as diverse as language, memory, listening, and physical and social skills. Music evokes both emotional and physical responses and offers many opportunities for enjoyable interactions, especially between children and adults. Participating in pleasurable and appropriate music experiences can also help children build self-confidence and self-esteem.

One of the most creative means of teaching expectations is to change the lyrics of a popular song. Research in the neurosciences supports the idea that encoding text into a familiar melody helps an individual remember the material; words presented by song are remembered significantly better than when presented by speech. Think of your favorite advertising jingle. Chances are that you can sing it, even if you have not heard it in several years.

Here is a simple illustration of how professionals can use the lyrics of popular songs to teach expectations. One of the most well-known songs for children is "If You're Happy and You Know It." Simply replace the word *happy* with the desired expectation:
If you're being safe and you know it, clap your hands. (clap, clap)
If you're being safe and you know it, clap your hands. (clap, clap)
If you're being safe and you know it, then your face will surely show it.
If you're being safe and you know it, clap your hands. (clap, clap).

SUPPORTING A POSITIVE CLASSROOM COMMUNITY

Provide an environment where young children can feel safe, supported, and welcome, giving them a desire to explore and learn from their experiences. Following is a list of strategies that can support a positive classroom community:

■ **Daily schedule:** Post a clearly understandable daily schedule, and use and refer to it throughout the day. By knowing what is coming next, children will learn a sense of time and organization, as well as the security of knowing the regular sequence of events. It is very important that children know that their basic needs, such as having the opportunity to eat, will be taken care of. If children know when and where they will eat every day, no matter what, then they will be able to focus on what the teacher wants them to do.

89

■ **Responsibility charts:** Create a responsibility chart using the children's names, classroom jobs, and pictures of the children next to their responsibilities. Almost every young child can identify his picture on a chart. One of the goals of any good early childhood program is to teach independence. Responsibility charts allow young children to feel a great sense of empowerment, and children who feel empowered are more likely to enjoy the program.

Students often forget their classroom responsibilities and have to be reminded. Having a responsibility chart takes the burden off the early childhood professional and places responsibility on the children. In addition, responsibility charts build a sense of community, belonging, and ownership, which are critically important aspects of any early childhood environment. Finally, responsibility charts prevent challenging behavior associated with conflicts over classroom jobs.

- **Community gatherings:** During community gatherings, the teacher, teacher assistant, and children come together as a group. They develop trust and acceptance as they share, learn, listen, and participate in meaningful activities. A community gathering that follows predictable patterns consistently throughout the year allows young children to gain confidence by knowing what to expect.

  It is crucial that the early childhood staff considers guidelines to prevent challenging behaviors from occurring. The length of group time is determined by the age and developmental level of the children; the younger the children, the shorter the group time. At the beginning of the year, group time for young children may last only 10 minutes and may possibly increase to a maximum of 15 minutes. Have clear objectives for each group activity, and gather all needed materials in advance so the flow of the activity is not disrupted. Create a balance of activities that includes listening, singing, discussing, and moving. Young children will provide important feedback that can help you determine whether to shorten or lengthen an activity.

  The community gathering area needs to be the largest center in your classroom. This will provide young children enough space to prevent disruptive behavior, especially related to spatial boundaries, from occurring. Adults can provide a variety of materials to establish spatial boundaries in the large group area, such as carpet squares, tape, Hula-Hoops, or even handkerchiefs. In addition, early childhood teachers can use placemats as personal space markers. The placemats are easy to clean and enable the teacher to print or place a child's picture on the mat to predetermine seating arrangements.

- **Manipulative materials:** Young children need the opportunity to engage with a variety of manipulative materials because this activity assists in developing their fine motor skills and finger dexterity, which lead to writing skills. In addition, the materials assist young children with focusing on the activity at hand, sustaining their attention, and remaining in one location instead of wandering the classroom. Include lots of materials that can be used in a variety of ways to give children a sense of creativity and control. Provide a few containers of different manipulatives to encourage a smooth transition as the child enters the program in the mornings.

- **Closed-ended materials:** Closed-ended materials, such as a jigsaw puzzle, wooden counting disks, knobbed cylinder blocks, nesting towers, and carousel shape sorters, have only one correct solution. The advantage of having such materials in an early childhood program is that, when completed, they provide young children with instant success. Young children often need to experience that sense of gratification.

- **Sensory materials:** Teachers can never have too many sensory materials in the classroom. These items provide a strong sense of calm and relaxation when young children interact with them. Provide water and sensory tables, along with a separate sensory center where young children can experience a variety of materials. Children can use sand, water, playdough, or other sensory materials in a variety of ways, depending on their maturity, ability, past experience, interest, and involvement. Throughout the year, the following materials can be rotated in the sensory table: sand, dirt, white mud (1 roll of white toilet paper, 1 bar grated Ivory soap, and warm water), Styrofoam peanuts, confetti, shredded paper, cornstarch and water, shaving cream, ice, cotton balls, capsaicin-free birdseed, smooth pebbles, and sawdust. Young children who are hypersensitive to touch need the opportunity to experience a variety of sensory materials to obtain the stimulation their brain needs. Thus, they need sensory materials that provide soothing and comforting tactile experiences.

- **Calming areas:** The classroom needs soft areas that children can select when they need some time alone or quiet time. Create a womblike effect by enclosing the area on three sides; small tents, teepees, and large boxes work well. Alternatively, you can create a similar effect by hanging a sheet, fishnet, or parachute from the ceiling at a height of about 4 feet from the floor. Use

WHEN NOTHING ELSE WORKS

a variety of soft materials, such as rugs, beanbag chairs, pillows, blankets, sleeping bags, or a mattress, to furnish the area. To help children release energy in a positive manner, you may wish to include playdough, a slinky toy, stress balls, bubble wrap, or flexible figures as well.

- **Post office center:** All of us enjoy receiving mail from friends and loved ones. Consider creating a classroom post office and incorporating it as part of the morning transition. Encourage families to visit the post office center at drop-off time and to write a brief note to their child. They can place their notes in envelopes and drop them in the "mailbox." Later in the day, the mailperson can deliver the mail to the child whose name appears on the envelope. Most young children are excited to receive their letters and immediately want them opened and read to them.

  This concept not only encourages literacy but also creates a positive emotional state for the young child and provides a wonderful opportunity for families to encourage prosocial behavior. Consider extending the strategy as part of the nap-time routine. The mailperson could deliver the letter before nap time, and the adults could read the positive messages to the children as they lie on their cots.

  One Head Start program linked this strategy with their family-involvement and home-visit programs. When instructors visited the home of a child, they brought self-addressed, stamped postcards with them. Families could then write messages on the postcards and mail them back to the center on a weekly basis. Instructors placed the postcards into the post office center's mailbox, and they were delivered to the young children later that day.

- **Positive journal:** A positive journal is a strategy based on the principles of positive psychology. Families of young children who display challenging behaviors often receive feedback on their children's inappropriate behavior but are granted very few reports on their child's positive, prosocial behaviors. Because of these interactions, a negative attitude begins to develop among everyone involved.

  The positive journal attempts to develop nurturing interactions between the families and centers by having the early childhood professional document three positive behaviors the young child

93

displayed during the day. It is important to document the examples as soon as they occur, since they may be difficult to remember at the end of the day. Before the young child leaves the center, review and acknowledge the three positive behaviors noted throughout the day. After the discussion, place the positive journal in the student's backpack so families have the opportunity to review and acknowledge the prosocial behavior at home. It is interesting to note that families often will begin to write down their own observations about their child's behavior to be shared with the early childhood professional via the positive journal.

The classroom environment and how it is set up may prevent challenging behaviors from occurring. Young children need predictability and stability in their lives, and the classroom environment will communicate these important elements. Throughout this chapter, I have provided specific ideas to incorporate into the learning environment that will help reduce challenging behaviors and will give every child the opportunity to flourish.

WHEN NOTHING ELSE WORKS

PREVENTION

Just as you can change your fixed mindset to a growth mindset, there are specific strategies that you can implement in your program to assist children in developing a growth mindset. These strategies not only apply to young children but also can be used with older students.

Helping Children Develop a Growth Mindset

Focus on the Struggle

When a child is learning something new and is getting annoyed and frustrated, the temptation is to take away the thing that is causing so much distress or to complete the task for the child. This is not a good idea, unless the activity is truly beyond the child's developmental stage. The better option is to focus on the struggle and why it is important. For example, if the child is aggravated during the learning process, you can help her persevere by using statements such as, "That is a struggle. You're learning how to do it."

Statements like these communicate to the child that you understand both the difficulty and the importance of perseverance in learning. Learning can be a frustrating business. Taking away the opportunity for children to learn something on their own is robbing them of opportunities to grow. Think of ways you can encourage children to enjoy the challenge inherent in learning.

Set Realistic Goals

Children must learn skills such as eating with a fork and knife, assembling a toy, or building a tower with blocks by taking small steps. If they do not master skills instantly, it does not mean they will never learn them.

Expecting too much of them can undermine their willingness to learn and behave because they may not be able to succeed in these difficult tasks if they are not yet developmentally ready. Learning takes time. Set realistic, achievable goals and celebrate the small successes in the learning process.

Offer Specific Feedback

Children need a tremendous amount of immediate feedback from the caring adults in their lives. Praising a child for fixed traits such as intelligence or ability or praising him too generally gives the child no useful tools to get better at what he is doing. Not only does it give him no helpful information, but it also undermines his motivation and love of learning because you are acknowledging something the child cannot change. You are sending the message that you value ability rather than hard work, effort, or perseverance.

Instead, use specific feedback that identifies the child's effort. One form of feedback is encouragement—for example, "You were able to remain on your carpet square for the entire story." All children need immediate feedback to assist in developing the neuron connections within the frontal cortex that are associated with self-regulation, including decision making. Acknowledging effort can encourage the young child to keep up his efforts in the future.

And although giving feedback is important, be careful not to micromanage. It is very easy to give children feedback on every positive thing they do and to interrupt their play to give them praise. If a child is engrossed in play, leave her to it. You will probably have to fight the urge to jump in, but if you interfere, it will break her concentration and undermine valuable learning. Giving feedback on everything a child does is unnecessary and may lead to diminished motivation. Think about it: if you were engrossed in something, would you want someone giving you feedback on everything you did? This also may encourage children to do only those things that require feedback. They then learn to rely on extrinsic feedback rather than their inner resources and internal motivation.

Ask open-ended questions to lead a child to solve a problem or achieve a goal: "What do you think will happen if..." or "Why do you suppose..." These questions build logical thinking skills and often lead to rich discovery.

ENCOURAGE RISK TAKING

Watch and listen to the child so you can take cues about what else she is ready to tackle. Psychologist Lev Vygotsky calls this the *zone of proximal development,* when we gently encourage children to use what they know to try something just a bit out of their reach but developmentally appropriate. By offering small but achievable challenges, we help children become confident and persistent.

MODEL PERSISTENCE

Be persistent and growth oriented yourself. Narrate your thoughts as you try something new or frustrating. Children might even be able to offer you some helpful tips. By modeling and thinking aloud, you will allow children to see that we all have to work hard to solve problems and that we all continue to learn new things.

DON'T SWEAT THE SMALL STUFF

Accidents and mistakes happen. Show the children that we can learn, even when we do not achieve what we set out to accomplish. We may learn that we need help from someone else or that we should return to the task at another time. We may learn that we need to break the task down into smaller steps. When faced with an unsuccessful attempt, be specific about what worked, identify the emotions involved, and offer encouragement for the next time.

DEVELOPING TRUST AND NOURISHING RESPECT

Merriam-Webster's Collegiate Dictionary defines *trust* as "assured reliance on the character, ability, strength, or truth of someone or something." Trust is a critical issue because a relationship without trust is not really a relationship at all. Research shows that trust is the basis for creating a predictable, stable, and nurturing environment.

Trust for children refers to the sense that the world is a safe place, filled with caring and nurturing people. Trust is the first level in Erik Erikson's model of social and emotional development and is one of a child's fundamental psychological needs.

Because of the changes in society and the family, children often are mistrusting instead of trusting. The messages children receive from many television and video games are that the world is not safe but is a scary and dangerous place to live. In addition, many children have directly experienced neglect or violence.

The development of trust in children is based on love, acceptance, respect, encouragement, and freedom to experiment and make mistakes. Being consistent and nurturing are two of the most important qualities adults can offer to help a child develop trust. Children coming from chaotic environments may need more time with routines and consistency in order to begin to trust you and others. Since they are not accustomed to limits or routines, expect these children to test the limits to see whether the adult will be consistent and follow through on what she says.

Trusting relationships help people through vulnerable times of change and risk taking and contribute to people's identity and motives for action. Many of today's children are starved for access to adults, rich life experiences, and belief in themselves. Often, their unpredictable home environments have not included a trusting relationship with another person. Act as a model of a healthy relationship, offering personal support so students can find meaning from their new learning and become effective members of the community.

PROVIDE A SAFE AND SECURE ENVIRONMENT

It is essential that children feel protected, safe, and secure in their learning environment. Ensure that all basic needs are met, including love, care, and physical closeness. Providing a safe environment where children want to explore and can learn from their exploration is the underlying principle of brain-based learning. Set the stage by creating a child-centered environment based on developmentally appropriate activities, expectations, and techniques, and organized to address positive discipline.

ENCOURAGE POSITIVE RELATIONSHIPS

Positive relationships in the classroom are in many ways prerequisites for effective learning and behavior. Research shows that positive and caring relationships increase resilience and protect children from failure, mental illness, drug and alcohol abuse, and destructive behavior or violence.

Effective teaching loses some of its impact when positive teacher-student relationships are lacking.

Even though the teacher and the child are responsible for their own behavior, the teacher is more capable of change and has more behavioral choices at her disposal than the child does. Therefore, teacher change—improving the environment or the relationship, altering responses to behavior, or changing the perception of the child or problem—is more advantageous than solely focusing on changing the child.

SUPPORT POSITIVE INTERACTIONS

The trusting teacher views all interactions with children, including interactions involving disciplinary or corrective measures, as opportunities to strengthen the teacher-student relationship. Most experts agree that to prevent misbehavior and develop a positive environment there should be three to five positive interactions for every negative interaction in the classroom.

PRACTICAL AND SPECIFIC STRATEGIES THAT PROMOTE TRUST

The following strategies help students develop trust in their teachers and classmates:

1. Listen with genuine interest and respect and without judgment. For example, you might say, "It doesn't matter whether or not I agree, but I am curious to hear your story."
2. Express affection and appreciation. For example, offer "When you. . ., then . . ." types of compliments, such as, "When you helped put away the blocks, you were being a thoughtful classmate."
3. Confront others lovingly. For example, say, "I don't know what your intent was, but the effect on me is . . .."
4. Reframe statements and ask questions to encourage people to open up and share more. Consider that what you call failure may be resilience. Ask *what* and *how* questions; avoid *why* questions. For example, you may observe a child having a tantrum because another child has taken the object he had in his hand. So you may ask him, "What happened to make you feel that way?" or "How did he make you feel when he took your toy?"
5. Emotion is the most important factor in any communication and controls the message that is being given. Any feeling is okay, but any action must be respectful and acceptable behavior.

Evaluate the trust in your program. How much trust is there between children and adults? Can children count on their teachers and peers in the class? Learning to trust one another and knowing you can rely on fellow students are important elements that encourage the class to work together as one.

TRUST ACTIVITIES

There are two ways to implement blindfolded trust in your program. First, have everyone find a partner. One person stands with his back to the other person, extends his arms forward as if he were driving a car, and closes his eyes. The partner stands behind this person and, without touching the blindfolded person, directs him around the room using verbal commands.

A variation of this activity is to have the partner physically direct the individual. The partner places her hands on the shoulders or hips of the blindfolded person. She physically guides the blindfolded person around the classroom.

FALLING BACKWARD

Note: To keep all participants safe, the falling backward activity must take place on a carpet or mat while participants are on their knees.

Partners kneel on a mat, and one lets herself fall backward and is caught by the other person. Initially, the catcher assumes a supportive position about one foot away from the person who is falling. After the initial fall, this activity can be repeated with a slightly greater separation between the partners.

SCULPTURING

Sculpturing is not only a wonderful activity to develop trust but also helps children grasp concepts associated with literacy and numeracy. Individuals pair up and stand facing each other. One of the partners pretends to be a hunk of clay. The other person is the sculptor whose responsibility is to sculpt her partner into a letter of the alphabet. Once the individual is sculpted into that letter, he must try to name the letter that his body represents. For young children who are learning the alphabet, limit the letters to just a few that the children know. If the children know their letters, increase the challenge by asking the sculpted person to provide the phonetic sound the letter makes.

Another variation of this activity is to sculpt numbers instead of letters. This activity not only develops trust between the participants but takes learning numbers and letters to a whole new dimension by creating them with the body.

GRAPHO

Grapho not only promotes trust but also encourages the development of letter and number recognition. In this activity, children pair up, and one of the children traces a letter on the other child's back. The partner then attempts to guess which letter has been drawn on his back. A variation of this activity is to have the children trace a letter or number in the palm of the other child's hand as he looks away. Not only does this activity help to develop trust among participants, but it also introduces a tactile sensory component to learning numbers and letters.

BACK ART

Back art focuses on communication but also is an excellent activity that centers on learning pre-academic concepts. Divide the class into groups of five or six. Have each group sit, back to front, in a single-file line facing the front of the room. The last person from each line meets with the teacher, who privately shows them a letter, number, or picture to draw. After seeing the picture, they go back to their spots at the ends of their team lines. At the starting command, the end person uses one finger to trace the picture the teacher showed him onto the back of the child in front of him. The person in front of him then draws the same thing on the back of the next person in line. Alternatively, the person can draw on a piece of paper held against the child's back. This continues until reaching the first person in line, who tries to draw on a piece of paper what she thinks was drawn on her back. After all teams have finished, the first person in each line holds up her drawing for the team and class to see how well the team did. The teacher should hold up the original so the drawings can be compared.

103

The teams may not ask questions about what is being drawn on their backs as the activity progresses. They should also be encouraged not to look at the other teams to see what they are drawing. The pictures you choose to have them draw should be fairly simple but related to vocabulary development. Some suggestions are a star, house, flower, tree, boat, letter of the alphabet, happy face, sun, numbers, and so on.

REMOTE-CONTROL DRAWING

Remote-control drawing provides instant feedback to children as they write or draw different letters, numbers, pictures, or words. Children pair up in this activity. One of the children will hold the writing instrument in her dominant hand while the other child will place his hand on top of his partner's hand and writing instrument, thus controlling the hand and writing instrument to draw whatever number, letter, word, or object has been requested. If the child controlling the hand and writing instrument begins to incorrectly produce the item, the individual holding the writing instrument may give him immediate feedback by resisting drawing the item.

A variation of this activity is to have the children switch roles and, instead of using their dominant hand, both children will use their nondominant hand to engage in the activity. By using the nondominant hand, children will engage the other hemisphere of their brain for learning.

DICTATED DRAWING

Dictated drawing focuses on listening and auditory processing. This activity also uses premath concepts and language to describe the object being drawn. In this activity, the adult or a child gives verbal directions on how to draw an object or picture that is in front of her but is shielded from the rest of the group. Based on the description of the object, each person in the group tries to draw the object. The one who is describing may not use any gestures or other nonverbal communication. At the end of the activity, the describer shares the object with the group so the listeners can see the item they were attempting to draw.

FOLLOW THE FOLLOWERS

Follow the followers helps children develop self-control while focusing on visual and auditory clues. To begin the activity, have seven children stand shoulder to shoulder in a line. Next, have every other person face the opposite direction, still remaining shoulder to shoulder. This means that if the first person is facing forward, the next person would face backward, the third person would remain facing forward, and so on. The first person (who can also be the adult) tells the followers they will all jump one foot forward at the same time on his signal. The leader says, "Jump!" and all of the followers jump forward. The followers return to the original line, continuing to face in opposite directions. Next, the leader explains that all the followers will jump at the same time the leader jumps, but with no auditory cues. The leader jumps and all the followers follow.

MIRRORING

Mirroring is a way of honing skills of self-regulation and concentration. It can be used to help the group bond and develop that instant communication so necessary for building trust. It teaches careful observation skills, which serve children in all aspects of their increasingly complex lives. Plus, it is a lot of fun!

Everyone takes a partner, and if there is an odd number, the teacher pairs with someone. Partners stand facing each other, about one to three feet apart. One is the leader and the other is the mirror. Moving only from the

105

waist up, the leader makes simple gestures or movements. The mirror duplicates the leader's movements exactly—just as a mirror would. Some children may have trouble with the right-left shift. If the leader raises her right hand, the mirror should raise his left, just as the figure in a real mirror would.

Once you have all the children concentrating on mirroring, have them switch leaders a few times. At first, every time they switch leaders they will need to start over, but they should reach the point where they can switch leaders in midstream, without interrupting the smooth flow of movement. Eventually this exercise can grow to involve the whole body and even locomotion, but be wary of beginning this too soon.

Feather Painting

Feather painting is a variation of face painting, an activity that is always a popular attraction at fairs, festivals, and celebrations. Have the child close his eyes, then gently begin "painting" his face with a craft feather. You can also have the child paint your face or other children's faces in the group.

Stroking

Stroking is one of the higher-level trust activities because it involves touch surrounding personal-space issues.

Since this activity involves touching, it is important to know your program policy on contact with young children. In addition, you must know your children well before you undertake this exercise. If a child has been sexually abused or has sensory processing disorder, this activity could produce an adverse reaction. It is only recommended for children or groups who can conduct the activity in a mature way.

Tactile stimulation is one of the most important ways to communicate to a young child. It is essential that young children feel secure and develop a basic sense of trust. Touching will convey kindness, security, and calmness. As parts of the body are touched, the child will develop a sense of body awareness, which is essential for sensory integration.

In this activity, children pair up. One of the children is the receiver and stands still while the other child strokes his back or arm or another body part as directed by the adult. It is important to demonstrate for the children beforehand that a downward stroking motion is relaxing to the receiver. For the next level, have the children switch positions. This time the receiver closes his eyes, not knowing which body part the stroker will address. Instead of announcing the body part to be stroked to the entire group, as the strokers look on, the adult points to the specific body area to be stroked.

Helping Hands

The helping hands activity is a game that was commonly played on *Whose Line Is It Anyway?*, a popular television show hosted by Drew Carey. In this activity, the children pair up. One child stands in front of the other, with her back to that child. The child in front places her hands in her front pockets or behind her back. Since the child in front is not able to use her hands, the person standing behind provides the arms for the child by placing her own arms under the front child's armpits. Once the children are in position, they can engage in a variety of fine motor activities such as zipping a coat, eating, drinking, or sensory play. It may be beneficial to have the child in front wear a smock.

Using Active Learning to Prevent Challenging Behavior

As early childhood educators know, learning is not an automatic consequence of pouring information into a child's head. It requires the learner's own mental involvement and experience. Explanation and demonstration alone will never lead to real, lasting learning; only active learning will do this.

When learning is active, children do most of the work. They study ideas, solve problems, and apply what they learn. To learn something well, it helps to hear, see, ask questions, and discuss it with others. Above all, students need to experience—figure things out by themselves, come up with examples, practice skills, and complete assignments that depend on the knowledge they already have or must acquire. Active learning is fast-paced, fun, supportive, and personally engaging. Often, children are out of their seats, moving about and thinking out loud.

NOURISH RESPECT IN CHILDREN

The following suggestions will help you develop respect with the children in your program:

- Listen carefully when children speak.
- Remain open minded and objective.
- Consider children's messages carefully.
- Avoid interrupting a child or offering unsolicited advice or criticism.
- Respect children's personal space. Children may feel threatened and become agitated if you violate their personal space. When you attempt to physically restrain children, you affect their level of trust and respect in you and other adults.

- Use friendly gestures, not aggressive ones. Avoid using a finger-pointing gesture. Open, upturned palms may be more appropriate and effective.
- Use the child's preferred name. Ask each child how he would like to be addressed in the classroom. Only in rare instances would his chosen name be inappropriate.
- Get on their level. If the child is seated, try kneeling or bending over, rather than standing over her.
- Ask questions rather than make accusations. This assumes that the child is a responsible person: "Are you ready to begin?" rather than "Put your book away. It's time to start group." Use a concerned and kind tone.
- Address problem behaviors privately. Reprimanding children in front of their peers may embarrass them unnecessarily. Speaking to them privately helps preserve their integrity and self-esteem.

ACTIVE LEARNING CREDO

What I hear, I forget.
What I hear and see, I remember a little.
What I hear and see, ask questions about, or discuss with someone else, I begin to understand.
What I hear and see, discuss, and do, I acquire knowledge and skill from.
What I teach to another, I master.

When young children are engaged in active learning, there are fewer opportunities to engage in challenging behavior because the functions of that behavior are being met. For example, when children are passively sitting in a circle listening to the teacher discuss numbers, they easily become bored and begin to engage in inappropriate behavior to gain attention or escape the mundane activity. However, if the children have the opportunity to engage in the discovery of numbers at different centers that incorporate the concepts into their activities, the children actively learn about numbers.

In addition, when children have choices in how, where, what, and when they want to learn, they have fewer opportunities for power struggles leading to adult-child conflict. Adults who understand children's need to be active become involved in supporting and extending children's self-initiated activities rather than trying to control children's behavior. For example, when adults encourage children to talk about their choices and decisions, children will speak freely and express their wants, needs, and desires instead of acting out behaviors that may be interpreted as disruptive. When adults eliminate long periods of waiting and listening in favor of active learning experiences, children direct their energies toward working with the materials they have selected rather than engaging in disruptive behavior. An active learning environment provides a climate where learning is enjoyable and engaging for children.

ENCOURAGING ACTIVE LEARNING

To encourage active learning in your program, the High/Scope Educational Research Foundation suggests five key ingredients that capture the essence of active learning in an early childhood program:

- **Materials:** Provide abundant, age-appropriate materials that the child can use in a variety of ways. Learning grows out of the child's direct actions on the materials.
- **Manipulation:** Offer the child opportunities to explore, manipulate, combine, and transform the materials chosen.
- **Choice:** Let the child choose what to do. Since learning results from the child's attempts to pursue personal interests and goals, the opportunity to choose activities and materials is essential.
- **Language from the child:** Listen as the child describes what he is doing. Through language, the child reflects on his actions, integrates new experiences into an existing knowledge base, and seeks the cooperation of others in their activities.
- **Adult support:** Recognize and encourage the child's reasoning, problem solving, and creativity.

USING ACTIVE SUPERVISION TO PREVENT CHALLENGING BEHAVIORS

MIS (Moving, Interacting, and Scanning) strategy is a component of active supervision associated with the Positive Behavior Support model. Active supervision is a specific method for monitoring children in classroom transitions and in nonclassroom settings. Researchers have found active supervision to be effective in both decreasing inappropriate behaviors and increasing appropriate behaviors in learning environments.

Active supervision is defined by its three behaviors—moving, interacting, and scanning—which increase adult awareness and heighten responsiveness to child activity. Active supervision is a good way to promote child safety and well-being in a program.

- **Moving** consists of walking around the setting, visiting problem areas often, and making your presence known to the children. Instead of using a regular pattern, move unpredictably so children will not know where or when you will be in direct proximity.

- **Interacting** includes teaching expectations and talking with children informally. Interaction allows you to build a positive relationship with children, prevent inappropriate behavior, and emphasize positive behavior.
- **Scanning** is a technique used to examine the environment frequently, looking for both appropriate and inappropriate behaviors. This allows you to be aware of all the behaviors children are displaying during transitions. Teachers who use scanning effectively glance around the classroom regularly, looking for multiple opportunities to acknowledge children behaving appropriately.

Adults can use MIS strategy to provide consistent and preventive monitoring of children's behaviors, especially during transitions when there may be changes in staff, settings, and behavioral expectations.

Using Physical Movement to Prevent Challenging Behavior

Providing children with appropriate ways to channel their energy can prevent behavioral problems from developing, can build self-confidence, can improve physical health, and can make learning fun.

From a physiological standpoint, all bodies are designed to move. The body has obvious, positive responses to movement. When engaged in physical activity, people of all ages typically experience pleasure. As a result of movement, the brain releases neurotransmitters, such as serotonin and dopamine, and hormones, such as endorphins and adrenaline, which promote pleasure and excitement.

Recent research in the neurosciences has discovered that there are many purposes for movement:
- Preparing the brain with specific movements may improve communication from one part of the brain to another.
- Providing brain breaks can give the brain the opportunity it needs to process and consolidate information.
- Developing class cohesion through movement activities can prepare the brain for learning new information.
- Reviewing and teaching content through movement will help students of all ages and cultures to understand and retain information.

Most children do not do well sitting still and listening for a significant amount of time. Children learn better and are happier when they can move around, touch, and manipulate things. When children who thrive on moving and touching have to sit for extended periods of time, disruptive behaviors occur. Teachers become confused, frustrated, and angry because these children do not learn or behave like their classmates. In turn, families are bombarded with negative reports: "Janie won't stay in her chair," or "Antwan won't sit on his carpet square."

A more serious concern is that many children are being misdiagnosed with attention deficit hyperactivity disorder, behavioral disorder, or oppositional defiant disorder because they simply have a need to move. One way to reduce the number of these false positives is to create environments that give children opportunities to move.

Some children are kinesthetic learners; they best absorb information by moving and physically experiencing the material they are trying to learn. Sitting still while trying to absorb new information can be frustrating, and kinesthetic learners typically will introduce some form of movement into the activity. Fidgeting, wiggling, kicking, and touching are all indications that a child needs more physical activity to effectively process data.

Early childhood environments can be stressful not only for the adults but also for children. These stressors can come from many areas, including extended days, prolonged sitting, conflicts with peers, and unmet needs. Movement can have a positive effect on the brain because it reduces the release of the stress hormone cortisol, which helps reduce stress levels and thus prevents behavioral problems from occurring. Cross-lateral movements, in particular, are highly beneficial for boosting learning and keeping the brain and body functioning well. Cross-lateral movements are those in which arms and legs cross over from one side of the body to the other. The left side of the brain controls the right side of the body, and the right side of the brain controls the left side. Both sides are forced to communicate when arms and legs cross over.

SIMPLE CROSS-LATERAL MOVEMENTS

Cross the midline: Stand upright. With the right hand touch the left knee, and then with the left hand touch the right knee. Do the same with bent elbows.

Walking the eight: Use two large plastic hoops or tape to construct an eight in the classroom, or use chalk to draw a figure eight outside. Ask the children to walk the entire figure eight. Modify the movements to include hopping, skipping, jumping, or galloping.

Nose-ear: With the right hand, tap the left earlobe while at the same time the left hand is touching the tip of the nose. Rest both hands for a few seconds in the lap before switching, putting the left hand to the right earlobe and the right hand to the tip of the nose.

Windmill: Stand with feet spread apart, and bend over at the waist. Tap the right hand on the left foot. Stand up straight, then bend over to tap the left hand to the right foot.

Backward: Bend the left knee and left foot up behind the right leg. Reach back with the right hand and touch the left foot. Repeat with the right foot and left hand.

Crossover sitting: Sit and cross the right leg over the left one. Bend the left elbow and touch the right knee. Repeat with the left leg and right elbow.

CHAPTER 6 ■ PREVENTION

These movements assist the child in developing self-regulation by providing communication between the two brain hemispheres through the corpus callosum. According to neuroscience research, the hormone levels of our bodies reach a peak about every 90 minutes. This can cause either of the hemispheres of the brain to get stuck. Cross-lateral movements are an efficient, easy way to get things moving again. They increase the blood flow in all parts of the brain, leading to increased energy levels and alertness. They also stimulate neurotrophin production, which spurs the building of synaptic connections, which are important for learning and self-regulation.

If a child has a trusting relationship with the adults in the program, the likelihood of the child displaying inappropriate behavior lessens. Many young children do not trust adults because of negative experiences in their pasts. The activities in this chapter are designed to develop trust, and a number involve movement because young children learn best when they are actively engaged. But, trust and movement on the part of the children are not enough; the adults must also actively supervise by remembering to scan, move, and interact.

INTERVENTION

Sometimes challenging behaviors continue to occur even after preventative strategies such as the ones discussed in previous chapters have been implemented. Following is a series of intervention strategies that focus on positive guidance and a child-centered approach that treats children with respect and dignity.

ACTIVE LISTENING

Children need to feel they are heard. In the early childhood program, sometimes it can be difficult to hear what a child has to say, and at other times it might be hard to get a child to talk about his thoughts and feelings at all. Active listening is a tool developed by Thomas Gordon that enables us to identify with a child's feelings, validate and interpret them, and demonstrate understanding and acceptance. In addition, active listening allows and encourages a child to communicate his needs. When young children feel accepted and trusted, they learn to accept and trust other people. Active listening not only promotes trust, but it also provides a sense that the adult cares and will do everything within her power to provide a safe and nurturing environment for the child.

Active listening is an excellent intervention strategy, especially if the challenging behavior is associated with an emotional reaction such as anger. The simple technique of identifying and validating a child's emotions can defuse anger, clarify needs, and open the child up to possible solutions.

The following script between Courtney and her teacher exemplifies active listening:

COURTNEY: (Walks into the classroom and throws her coat down)
TEACHER: *I see that you are upset.*
COURTNEY: *I hate this place.*
TEACHER: *I see that you are upset because you had to come to preschool.*
COURTNEY: (Kicks the cubby and shouts) *Adam gets to stay home with Mommy! It's not fair!*
TEACHER: *It's upsetting when your little brother gets to stay home with Mommy while you have to come here. Let's write a note to Mommy telling her how you feel, and then let's read the book* Mommy Don't Go *together.*

By using active listening, you can assist the young child in identifying her feelings and, most importantly, you help her understand why she is feeling that way. Active listening opens up the channels of communication and often helps children reveal the real reasons behind their emotional state.

To actively listen, the listener must concentrate on what the child is communicating, rather than thinking about the next point she is going to make. By following this guideline, active listening keeps adults from offering premature advice, criticism, commands, and other communications that often provoke defensiveness or extinguish communication.

Not only can you actively listen to the young child's words but also to the pitch and intensity of her voice and the rhythm of her delivery. In addition, her body language will give you an indication of how she feels. Be aware of the situation and the immediate environment the child has engaged in. The environment provides vital clues to why the child is feeling and behaving a certain way.

METACOMMUNICATION

Metacommunication is anything other than the words themselves that communicate or affect, positively or negatively, the message contained in the words. Metacommunication includes the intensity and inflection of the voice, rate of delivery, facial expression, accompanying gestures, body language, and personal space. *Suprasegmentals* is the term for the vocal effects that extend over more than one sound segment in an utterance: the pitch, volume, and rate of speech. Suprasegmentals combined with body language, personal space, and facial expressions create metacommunication, which greatly influences the effect of a verbal message on a listener. According to *Louder than Words: Nonverbal Communication* by Mele Koneya, the total effect of a message breaks down like this: 7 percent is verbal (words); 38 percent is vocal (volume, pitch, and rhythm); and 55 percent is body movements.

Research in neurosciences indicates that when an individual is upset, he cannot focus well on the other person's actual words, since the brain's frontal lobes are receiving less blood and the limbic system is activated. This research provides important guidance on how to intervene with children who are exhibiting challenging behavior associated with anger.

It is very important that you remain calm and in control. When someone is directing verbal defiance toward you, the natural tendency is to respond in a similar fashion; for example, if a child begins to shout at you, the automatic reaction is to raise your voice, too. Unfortunately, this

further activates the emotional centers of the brain, tells the angry child that she is under threat, and escalates her reaction. When you escalate, there is a change not only in your suprasegmentals but also in your metacommunication, such as body language. Your rhythm, voice volume, and pitch increase. However, when you respond calmly, there is a change in rhythm and a decrease in voice volume and pitch, which will have a calming effect on the child. Thus, when you communicate calmness through metacommunication, you assist the child in calming herself.

Use a calming tone of voice, avoiding tones that suggest impatience, disgust, or sarcasm. Moderate your volume—not too loud or too soft. Speak clearly and slowly. If you speak too rapidly or haltingly, your communication patterns convey agitation and loss of control. By speaking calmly and clearly, you are more likely to defuse the child's anger and to be heard.

Nonverbal communication such as body language, gestures, facial expressions, and personal space are the most important aspects of dealing with a person exhibiting challenging behavior. Use the following guidelines to facilitate a positive outcome:

1. Respect personal space. This is the area around a person in which he feels safe. For most people and situations, it is about two to three feet. Entering an upset person's personal space intensifies the threat and the emotional responsiveness that activates the fight-or-flight response. As a general rule, keep at least an arm's length away from a child to prevent escalation of challenging behavior.

2. Maintain an open stance. Slightly turn your body at an angle to the other person, since this stance is less threatening. Keep your hands

open and in plain view. Do not cross your arms or point your finger at the person.

3. Use eye contact and facial expression appropriate to the situation. Your face and eyes convey a direct message to the other person. Maintain general eye contact, but do not stare through the other person. Be aware of culture differences; for example, some ethnic groups consider it inappropriate to look directly at another when upset. Your facial expression should be serious but not angry or fearful.

ENCOURAGEMENT AND FEEDBACK

All children need immediate feedback to assist in developing the neuron connections within the frontal cortex that are associated with self-regulation, including decision making. Because of the amount of time children spend with television, Internet, and video games, they need a tremendous amount of immediate feedback by the caring adults in their lives.

One form of feedback is encouragement, the acknowledgement of a young child's effort. When a child feels that his effort is recognized and appreciated, he develops a desire to try harder in the future. You can also use encouragement before and during an activity to help the child improve his behavior; for example, "Show me how you can put your toys away" or "I know you can keep your hands and body to yourself as you walk down the hallway" acknowledges and reinforces the child's attempts to improve his behavior.

It is important to note that there is ongoing debate regarding praise and encouragement in early childhood literature. Praise and encouragement are not the same:

- **Encouragement focuses on effort.** Unlike praise, encouragement does not place judgment on student work or give information regarding its value. Instead of saying, "Joshua, I like the way you are sitting at the lunch table," the encouraging adult might say, "Joshua, you are sitting at the lunch table." Judgment about the behavior is reserved for Joshua.
- **Encouragement is specific and honest.** Encouragement focuses on improvement of the process rather than evaluation of a finished product. Instead of saying, "Good job," say, "You cleaned up the

dramatic play area by yourself." Sincere, direct comments delivered with a natural voice are encouraging. Using encouragement helps teachers avoid overused phrases such as, "Wow, terrific work!" or "That's beautiful." By being more specific and honest, teachers can avoid using contradicting gestures or body language such as frowning. Encouraging statements should be offered with honest feeling. They should be credible and varied to suit the circumstances.

- **Encouragement does not set children up for failure or comparison.** Praise such as, "Anton, you're such a nice boy," is not encouraging because it is impossible to be nice all the time. Instead, use a comment such as, "Anton, I noticed you shared with Carlos today." Anton is left to determine for himself if he was indeed nice. Encouragement promotes a growth mindset because the adult is not setting the child up for failure.

- **Encouragement helps students develop an appreciation of their own behaviors.** Statements such as, "You were patient in the way you waited your turn for the computer," help the child analyze her behavior and better appreciate her efforts.

Wise teachers provide feedback to children by encouraging their behavior as often as possible. In a later chapter, we will discuss other systems of acknowledgement.

IGNORING CHALLENGING BEHAVIOR

If the function of the challenging behavior is to obtain attention, then ignoring is an effective strategy. You can ignore any challenging behavior for attention as long as the behavior is not harmful to the child or others or dangerous enough to require other forms of intervention. Ignoring behavior is simply pretending that the behavior is not occurring. The adults and peers do not look at, talk to, or respond to the child until the inappropriate behavior ends. It is extremely difficult for children to ignore their peers' challenging behavior, especially in a group setting. Children will need to be instructed on how to ignore the undesirable behavior of others. There are three basic guidelines for ignoring:

1. Offer the child no recognition when she is exhibiting unacceptable behavior. Do not have eye contact, physical contact, or in any way acknowledge the child.

2. Be consistent with your approach. Ignoring once and paying attention the next time will likely increase the intensity of the behavior. The child will think she must escalate the behavior for you to respond.

Even when you are consistent in your approach, expect the intensity of the behavior to increase before it decreases.

3. Recognize the child as soon as the unacceptable behavior stops. Ignoring always must be combined with supporting and encouraging positive behaviors.

One of the main reasons ignoring does not work is that the child's behavior will become worse before it gets better. This fact causes many adults to abandon ignoring as an intervention technique. In addition, other adults in the program or peers may continue to recognize the behavior, jeopardizing the success of the strategy.

NATURAL AND LOGICAL CONSEQUENCES

Natural consequences are the best learning experiences for people of any age. A natural consequence occurs when adults do not intervene in a situation; rather, they allow the situation to teach the child. For example, when children refuse to eat, they become hungry. If people stay awake too late at night, they will be tired the next day. If a child runs in the classroom, he may fall and skin his knees. In each of these cases, the person learns from the natural consequences of his behavior. The experience becomes the teacher. Natural consequences provide the opportunity for a teachable moment as the adult helps the child see the connection between behavior and natural consequences.

Natural consequences always work, but at times, they can be too severe or too delayed to be effective. In these cases, use logical consequences. For example, if a child runs into the street, the natural consequence of that behavior is obviously unacceptable. Instead, not allowing the child to play outside for a period of time offers a more logical consequence. Failure to brush one's teeth will result in cavities. However, that natural consequence will occur too late to be a deterrent. Therefore, not allowing sweets to children who refuse to brush their teeth works more effectively.

Logical consequences teach children to accept responsibility for their mistakes and misbehavior. The secret of an effective consequence is its logical connection to the misbehavior. If a child breaks a window, it is not logical for her to lose television rights or endure a lecture, since neither of these responses is related to the behavior. Paying for a new window, however, is both logical and educational. In the classroom, sending a child to timeout is not logically related to an inappropriate behavior; thus, she does not learn from the experience. When children see a clear and reasonable relationship between their inappropriate behavior and the consequence, they may be more likely to control their behavior.

You can apply one of the following types of logical consequences to specific, inappropriate behavior:

■ **Related Corrective Consequences:** In many instances, inappropriate behaviors lend themselves to the application of related corrective consequences, such as having toys or privileges removed or not being allowed to participate in an activity. Whenever possible, these consequences should be applied immediately so that the child can most readily associate them with his misbehavior.

■ **Reparations and Restitution:** Having children attempt to repair the damage caused by their actions is another form of meaningful consequence. The child who has caused another person pain, injury, or loss through destructiveness can be called upon to repair or make up for the harm by doing something extra for the person who has been hurt: "Because you hit Chris and made him cry, now you need to do something nice for Chris. Maybe Chris can take your place as line leader today."

Restitution is a form of reparation that was developed by Diane Chelsom Gossen, based on William Glasser's concepts of choice theory and quality schools. This approach allows teachers to help children learn new behaviors that can be used in other situations. The child who is exhibiting challenging behavior can be strengthened, can develop self-understanding, and can become the kind of person he wants to be. Because it does not focus solely on the victim, restitution helps a child learn self-discipline and reclaim his self-esteem through learning to evaluate what he can do to fix his own mistakes. This approach also strengthens agreed-upon beliefs and values about how we treat others.

Restitution involves allowing a student to perform some service that corrects or makes amends for undesirable behavior. In that way, the energy students expend on misbehavior is channeled in more constructive directions. For example, if a child hits one of her peers, an example of restitution would be to engage in an action that would relieve the pain, such as obtaining a cool paper towel to place on the injured area.

Restitution can increase students' sense of responsibility and personal pride in the successful working order of their program. The redeeming, constructive value of the task is essential to restitution; it allows for the promotion of acceptable behavior. The following are guidelines for proposing restitution:

1. Match the restitution to the misbehavior.
2. Make restitution the more desirable of the two choices.
3. Choose a restitution task that has some redeeming or constructive value.

Restitution tasks should lead to a positive end result. When making restitution, students develop the habits of helping others and using their energies to build and create. They acquire a sense of ownership, pride in their program, and unity with their peers. Students make a personal investment in their program and are therefore less likely to damage it in the future.

■ **Immediate Practice of Alternative Behaviors:** Guiding a child in practicing an alternative appropriate behavior can be instructive, especially immediately after an unintentional aggressive act toward others. Guiding the child through the appropriate behavior can help her learn how to avoid hurting others: "Instead of hitting Chris, next time you want to play with a toy he has, you can ask him politely by saying, 'Chris, may I play with that when you are finished?'"

Whenever possible, children should participate in setting up classroom expectations and the related consequences for not following those expectations. Involving children in this way increases the educational benefit of using consequences. Also, it will improve children's understanding of how consequences work and their willingness to follow the procedures they helped design. Before applying any new expectations or consequences, children need to know the reasons behind them. Demonstrations and role playing the expectations and consequences will help achieve this goal.

When young children are involved in setting consequences, they may offer inappropriate suggestions, such as telling a parent who will then spank the child. Provide the children with feedback regarding the appropriateness of the consequence, especially when suggested consequences might place a child in danger or do not reflect the philosophy of the program.

123

VARIABLES THAT AFFECT COMPLIANCE

Compliance is the performance or termination of an action at the request of another person. In early childhood programs, compliance occurs when the child is asked to either complete an action or stop an action that might be harmful or disruptive to others—for example, "Please keep your feet to yourself," or "Walk to your cubby and get your coat."

If a child continually does not comply with an adult's requests, the adult needs to investigate the following scenarios:

1. Was the child able to hear the request?
2. Was the child able to listen to the request?
3. Was the child able to understand the request?
4. Was the child capable of performing the requested task?

If the teacher or caregiver rules out all of the above, then the child may be choosing not to comply with the adult's requests. Sam Goldstein, author of *Understanding and Managing Children's Classroom Behavior,* offers the following advice on gaining children's compliance:

- **Do not use a question format when giving a command.** For example, "Would you please pick up the book?" is less effective than "Pick up the book." The use of questions instead of direct requests reduces compliance, because a question gives the child the opportunity to say no and exhibit defiant and oppositional behavior.
- **Get close to the child.** The optimal distance for giving a command is three feet. It is better to make a request up close than from across the room. Interestingly, this optimal distance closely corresponds with boundaries of personal space previously discussed.
- **Look the child in the eyes and be at his level.** It is better to look into the child's eyes or ask him to look into your eyes than not to make eye contact. Establishing eye contact will provide essential nonverbal information such as facial expression to the child. It is important to note, however, that some children will not establish eye contact because of cultural norms or disabilities such as autism. In those cases, do not force eye contact.
- **Give the child time (five to ten seconds) to respond to the request.** During this short interval, do not converse with the child, restate the request, or make a different request. Simply look the child in the eyes, and wait for compliance. For children who have auditory processing concerns or for whom English is their second language, you may need to double or triple that amount of wait time.

- **Give short requests.** For example, if the adult says, "I need for you to put away the book, push in your chair, use the restroom, wash your hands, and sit down at the table for lunch," there is far too much information for the child to process in short-term memory. In most cases, the child will remember the last thing she hears. Break the list into short requests, and wait for compliance with each before giving the next request.
- **Reduce the volume of your voice.** When you begin to raise your voice, many children will tune you out. It is better to make a request in a normal but firm voice than by using a loud voice.
- **Speak calmly.** Emotional requests decrease compliance and make the situation worse. When you become emotional, the child responds in kind. This type of emotional response interferes with compliance.
- **Describe the behavior you want.** Requests that are positive and descriptive are better than ambiguous or global requests. For example, if the adult remarks, "You need to listen," the request is too general, and children will have difficulty complying. However, if your request describes what you want the children to do, there is a much better chance for compliance: "Your lips need to be closed, and your eyes need to look at me."
- **Demonstrate.** Children see and children do. About 75 percent of the information children receive is processed visually, while only 13 percent is processed aurally. Children listen with their eyes, so when the adult models what is expected or requested, children are more able to process the command and comply. For example, if you request that a child put away the blocks, help her process and comply with the directive by picking up the first block yourself.
- **Give more positive "start" requests than "stop" requests.** Children will comply with positive directives 80 percent of the time. For instance, if someone says, "Don't think about elephants," you automatically think of elephants. When a teacher remarks, "Don't run," he is automatically reinforcing the negative behavior. Instead, change the command to a positive: "Walk in the classroom."

ADDITIONAL INTERVENTION STRATEGIES

In addition to the previously mentioned strategies, the following tactics are effective in intervening with challenging behavior when it occurs:

- **Make eye contact:** Not only an excellent preventative strategy, eye contact also effectively works as an intervention strategy for challenging behavior. Many of us may remember the power of eye contact from when we were in school. When a teacher makes eye contact with a child, it is less embarrassing than if she calls out the child's name. In addition, eye contact establishes a bond between the teacher and child that provides support and guidance. In some cases, the only intervention that is required to discourage a challenging behavior from continuing is eye contact with the child.

- **Be in close proximity:** When a child exhibits challenging behavior, a teacher's close proximity can be an effective intervention. If you know from prior experience that a particular child exhibits challenging behavior during a specific transition or activity, stand or sit close to the child. The child might respond to supportive physical nearness, and your physical proximity can stop a challenging behavior and avert a possible crisis.

- **Model positive behavior:** Often, children's reactions to a particular situation are directly related to their previous experiences, and they are not aware of the appropriate response. Modeling appropriate responses enables children to learn by observation, especially when the teacher models appropriate behaviors for specific problematic situations. Children need continuous repetition, because they do not generalize information from one situation to another. In addition, modeling provides feedback that helps children develop the neuron web in the prefrontal cortex of the brain associated with self-regulation.

- **Reteach classroom expectations:** Sometimes children will forget expectations that had been established for the class because of their short memories and because their primary focus is on the here and now. As previously mentioned, with the constant bombardment of electronic media, children need constant feedback regarding their behavior. Reteaching classroom expectations provides that feedback. When a child forgets a classroom expectation, ask the child to restate the expectation. State expectations positively, so the child hears what he should be doing as opposed to what he should not be doing.

- **Regroup and restructure the activity:** Occasionally, the activity or the composition of the group leads to management problems. In these cases, the most appropriate intervention strategy is to restructure the activity or reformulate the group. For instance, as the

WHEN NOTHING ELSE WORKS

children assemble for story time, a teacher might observe an increase in physical activity among the group. Before reading the story, ask the children to engage in a movement activity. They can release the built-up energy, so they will be more attentive to the story.

■ **Offer the child choices:** It is important for children to have control in their lives. By giving children choices, we empower them to accept and develop self-control. Choices help to alleviate power struggles between the adult and child. In most instances, when children are given choices, they will pick the most appropriate option.

When giving children options, consider a sequence of choices. For example, if you encounter power struggles during the clean-up routine, offer the child two neutral choices first: "Chris, pick up the round block or the square block first. It is your choice." Then, if the child is still indecisive, you can offer him a choice with a positive reinforcer attached: "Chris, if you pick up the round block or the square block, you will be able to choose the block-building area first during choice time tomorrow." As a last resort, pair the choice with a consequence: "Chris, if I have to pick up the blocks for you, tomorrow you will not be able to play in the block-building area. That is your choice." Depending on the relationship you have with the family, the following option also could be an effective strategy: "Chris, either you start to clean up the blocks, or I'll have your mom or dad help you clean up the blocks when they come to pick you up. It is your choice."

■ **Redirect:** An effective technique, redirection works because the circumstances are changed, even though they are changed by an adult. When the adult gives reasons for the change, children can soon learn to redirect themselves. When disruptive or unacceptable behavior occurs in a setting, a similar but more acceptable substitute can almost always be found. If not, another motivating activity may work just as well. For example, if a child is having difficulty keeping his hands to himself at the sensory table, the adult can redirect him to the manipulative area where he still engages in activities involving his hands but has the opportunity to interact with the materials individually.

■ **Encourage self-removal from the group or situation:** This approach resembles redirection, but the child, not the adult, changes the circumstances. For self-removal to be effective, you need to work closely with the child and her peers so self-removal does not have the

CHAPTER 7 ■ INTERVENTION

stigma of punishment. A child commonly will remove herself from a situation to work through an impulse or to regain emotional control so she is able to have a calm reaction. In addition to calming down, the child might need a strategy or skill to handle the situation; for example, a child may voluntarily leave a situation and approach the teacher for assistance.

■ **Encourage peer tutoring:** The goal of peer tutoring is to help the individual interact more frequently and more positively with others in a peer group. Peer tutoring assists the individual in learning the expectations and routines of the classroom. In considering someone to be a peer tutor, consider the following points: Select a child who attends the program regularly, and choose a child who exhibits social skills and behaviors that are frequently appropriate.

In early childhood programs, peer models are effective with children whose challenging behavior's primary function is to obtain attention. If the adult comments or provides attention to the child exhibiting challenging behavior, that attention automatically reinforces the behavior to continue. However, if the child's peer is displaying appropriate behavior, the teacher can direct her attention to that child: "Adam, you are sitting with your legs crossed and hands in your lap. You must be ready for the story." Adam becomes a model for the child displaying challenging behavior. In addition, this child sees the attention given to Adam and might begin to display listening behavior because she wants that attention from the adult, too.

■ **Distract:** A highly powerful way to alter an emotional state, distraction gets its power by stopping the angry train of thoughts that produce the emotional and behavioral response. Distraction can be a good way to defuse challenging behavior. Humor, offering a preferred object or activity, or even a change of facial expression can be effective distractions.

Verbal distractions can work, too, but might not be as effective as physical ones, depending on the emotional state of the child. Try, for example, commenting on the child's clothes: "Natalie, those are cool shoes." When Natalie focuses on her shoes, she is distracted from the thoughts producing the emotional state associated with the challenging behavior.

WHEN NOTHING ELSE WORKS

If a verbal distraction is not successful, try offering a preferred item to a child when challenging behavior is occurring. The item is intended to distract the child from the conditions that provoke the challenging behavior. In some cases, it will draw the child into an alternative focus, distracting him from the thoughts that may be fueling the challenging behavior.

Consider engaging the child in active exercise. Active exercise can cool anger because it changes the body's physiology from the high-arousal state of anger to a low-arousal state. Employ therapeutic materials, for example, as the child's behavior begins to escalate: pull out a roll of bubble wrap, lay it out, and then step on the bubbles. The child will see this action and want to participate in the activity. In addition to engaging the child in an active exercise (stomping on the bubbles), you also will have distracted the thoughts that create the emotional state producing the challenging behavior.

129

- **Remove the group:** When a child becomes physically violent, it is appropriate to remove other children from the immediate vicinity. Have a contingency activity for the other children to engage in while you handle the outburst. A removal activity might include moving the other children to another center or part of the room, then having a discussion with the child displaying the disruptive behavior about positive ways to manage anger and work on appropriate social and communication behaviors.

When a child escalates into physically aggressive behavior, staff members must act swiftly to ensure the safety of everyone involved. In every case, the first priority of the intervention is to ensure that no one is hurt. The second priority is to respond in a manner that avoids reinforcing the child's out-of-control behavior.

- **Clear the room:** In the same way that most programs have fire and tornado drills to keep everyone safe, it may be appropriate for your program to develop a "room clear" plan to use when physically violent behavior escalates. Whenever possible, the preferred method for dealing with out-of-control behavior is to remove everyone else from the threat of violence. When a student begins exhibiting behavior that puts anyone in jeopardy, the teacher should follow an established routine, such as moving students to another part of the room, then, if the behavior continues to escalate, moving students to the hall.

Room clears are preferable to physical intervention for a number of reasons:
1. A room clear helps to ensure everyone's safety. When students clear the room, they are removed from the immediate threat of physical danger.
2. A room clear removes the audience. Peer attention is potentially reinforcing to the student.
3. Physical intervention is likely to result in injury to the adult or student and can result in heightening the emotional intensity of the situation. Some students may be positively reinforced for out-of-control behavior through the sheer intensity of the interaction with an adult during physical restraint.
4. Using a room clear helps the student learn to manage his own behavior more rapidly. When physical intervention is used to control student behavior, the student mistakenly learns to depend

on an adult to bring his behavior under control. This results in the student believing he is unable to change or control his behavior.

5. Physical intervention requires an adult who is larger and stronger than the student. If the adult is unable to restrain the student easily, the situation goes unresolved until someone else can be summoned. As time passes, the risk of injury to other students in the room becomes greater.

COMBINING INTERVENTION STRATEGIES

Even though specific intervention strategies can be effective by themselves, using them together can be more beneficial, depending on the challenging behavior being exhibited. For example, if Charles is hitting other children at the sensory table because he does not want to share the materials, the early childhood professional could employ a combination of the techniques discussed. Preventatively, it is important to understand the function of the challenging behavior. Why is Charles hitting other children at the sensory table? Once the reason for his behavior is

131

understood, the teacher can determine which intervention strategies to use. Depending on Charles' emotional state, she might want to use active listening skills and calming techniques if he appears agitated. From a preventative point of view, there may not be enough materials at the sensory table, or there might be too many bodies in such a confined space. If the challenging behavior is associated with a lack of self-regulation, and Charles has difficulty sharing the materials, a combination of the following intervention strategies might be effective:

- Review the expectations, especially those focusing on keeping the environment safe and being a team player, which emphasizes the sharing of materials.
- Use logical consequences, especially those associated with reparations.
- Use redirection and choices by guiding Charles to choose another activity in a different part of the room.

No matter how positive your mindset, how well your environment is organized, and how sound your prevention strategies are, there will be times that young children exhibit behaviors that concern you. This chapter provides specific interventions that you can employ when these behaviors occur. From active listening to logical consequences such as restitution, these interventions provide teachable moments for the children to learn from the experience.

WHEN NOTHING ELSE WORKS

CREATIVE STRATEGIES TO TRY WHEN NOTHING ELSE WORKS

You have established a positive learning environment, taught routines and expectations, and implemented the intervention strategies described in previous chapters. Yet, the challenging behavior has not significantly changed in intensity, frequency, or duration.

Now what?

When the creative strategies described in this chapter are used in the context of a psychological perspective, they can expand the options that early childhood professionals have in intervening with challenging behavior. I will explore a number of creative strategies; most use simple, easy-to-find materials or no materials at all.

The function, type, and cause or origin of the challenging behavior will help determine which creative strategy to implement. For example, if the challenging behavior is associated with a neurological disorder that results in hyperactivity, then use creative strategies that promote calmness. However, if the behavior is aggressive in nature, consider the creative strategies that assist children in developing empathy, such as dramatic play, classroom pets, or children's books.

FIDGETS

"Fidgets" are a variety of objects that can be very effective self-regulation tools; they are used to help calm the body and mind. Many children feel an uncontrollable urge to fidget and move around. This need for movement is often a distraction to both the child and to those near her. Fidgets allow the child to experience movement without having to actually get up and move around. Manipulating a fidget provides the tactile stimulation the mind is craving, which can calm the child and allow her to stay on task.

Children should have the opportunity to engage in activities and materials that help relieve tension, such as water, sand, or sensory play. Materials such as clay and playdough allow children to release aggressive feelings. Fidgets can be manipulated during story time, circle time, or whenever concentration and focus is needed.

Many different types of fidgets are available. Depending on an individual's unique sensory needs, certain fidgets will work better for some children than others. While one child may crave tactile input and need a bumpy fidget in order to focus, another child might need proprioceptive input and need a hard ball she can squeeze. Try various fidget toys to see which works best for a particular child. The following is a list of inexpensive fidgets:

Slinky	necklaces	glitter jar
beads	plastic worms	Wikki Stix
gel bags	combs	pipe cleaners
flexible figures	bubble wrap	craft feathers
stress balls	clay	

There is a host of other fidgets available in a range of prices. Just type "fidgets" into a search engine. In addition to the commercially marketed fidgets, you easily can construct a stress ball, glitter jar, or gel bag. The advantage of constructing your own fidget is that the child can assist and have a feeling of pride and ownership.

STRESS BALL

Materials
1 small balloon
1 larger balloon
sensory material such as birdseed, sand, or salt
scissors
glue
plastic funnel

Procedure
1. Cut the stem from the larger balloon.
2. Fill the larger balloon with a sensory material. Tip: Use a funnel to pour the material into the balloon.
3. Cut the stem from the smaller balloon, and stretch it over the larger balloon, covering the hole.
4. Repeat the procedure with as many balloons as you like. This provides addtional layers in case a child tries to peel back the edges.
5. Seal the last opening with glue.

CALMING VESSEL

Materials

10–20 ounce clear plastic bottle with cap

baby oil

water

food coloring

glue

trinkets, sequins, or small plastic toys

Procedure

1. Fill the plastic bottle with water. Leave a little room.
2. Add food coloring.
3. Add sequins, trinkets, shapes made from aluminum foil, or small plastic toys.
4. Add a few tablespoons of baby oil.
5. Replace the cap, and glue it securely in place.

GEL BAG

Materials

hair gel

glue

2 ziplock plastic bags

glitter or small erasers

Procedure

1. Put some hair gel in a plastic bag. Do not overfill–leave room for the gel to move around. Variation: Substitute silly putty or shaving cream for the gel.
2. Add glitter or small erasers.
3. Seal the bag with glue.
4. Place the first bag inside a second bag, and seal the second bag with glue.

WHEN NOTHING ELSE WORKS

Fidgets for Biters

One of the most challenging behaviors facing early childhood professionals is biting. Biter fidgets are safe objects a child can bite instead of biting other children. These are especially good for the child who needs oral stimulation. Most fidgets for biters are textured and some are even flavored, both of which add to the sensory input.

You might want to provide several types of fidgets for biters, depending on what the child prefers. In the preschool classroom, tools commonly used for oral motor exercises might work best. Fortunately, there are quite a few styles, colors, and flavors on the market, so you are sure to find one the child likes. Common ones include Chewy Tubes, Super Chews, and Chew Stixx.

Also, you can easily construct your own biter necklace. At the pet or aquarium store, you can purchase silicone tubing that is used for filters in fish tanks. Once you obtain the tubing, cut off a piece that will comfortably fit around the child's head like a necklace but not be a choking hazard. Secure the ends of the tubing and place the necklace over the child's head. When the child has the urge to bite, he can bite into the tubing instead of seriously injuring you, other children, or himself.

Weighted Stuffed Animals

Some children have difficulty remaining in one place. During group activities, they will squirm around on the

137

floor and constantly need to be reminded to sit on their carpet squares. A weighted stuffed animal is a simple intervention strategy to help a squirmy child calm down and focus. The weighted stuffed animal does not give the child the opportunity to move and wiggle, and the extra weight provides grounding for the child.

To make one, obtain a clean stuffed animal and cut an opening that can be sewn closed later. Remove most or all of the stuffing, depending on the size of the animal. Pour sand into the animal to provide weight, and stitch the hole closed. During group time or other activities that require remaining in a designated area, a child can hold the animal to comfort himself and provide stability and structure.

WIGGLE SEATS

Many children need to wiggle. Most of the time this is not a problem; however, during story time or other activities that require sitting still, you may want to consider a child's rocking chair, beanbag chair, or wiggle seat. A rocking chair allows the child to move without disturbing the children around him. A beanbag chair also permits the child to move about, plus the beans will massage the child's body, producing a calming effect. An added benefit of the beanbag chair is that the child needs to exert a considerable amount of energy just to remove himself from it.

There are quite a few types of wiggle seats. Most of these are either wedges or round disks that are usually covered with bumps. Simply put one of these wedges or disks on a child's seat; then, have the child sit on it. He can wiggle his bottom all he wants, and he will not disturb those around him.

A small beach ball is an alternative to the commercially marketed wiggle seats. You can adjust the amount of air in the ball to produce the desired effect. Once the ball is partially inflated, placed it on the chair or in the area where the child will be sitting.

CLASSROOM PETS

Numerous studies support the positive effects of pets on children. One such study by the College of Nursing at the University of Nebraska Medical Center examined the effects of pets on physiological arousal and behavioral distress in preschool children (Nagengast, Baun, Megel, and Leibowitz, 1997). This study found that the presence of a pet reduced blood pressure, heart rate, and behavioral distress in the children. Children have a great need to nurture and to be nurtured; provide daily opportunities for these types of interactions. Caring for animals helps children develop a sense of responsibility, compassion, and empathy. Children and adults alike can benefit from interacting with pets, which can be a source of calmness and relaxation as well as a source of stimulation for the brain and body. Playing with a pet can even be a doorway to learning for a child, stimulating imagination and curiosity. Caring for an animal friend can also offer another benefit to a child: immense joy. Fish, hermit crabs, hamsters, gerbils, guinea pigs, and rabbits make excellent pets for early childhood programs.

Pets are never critical and do not give orders. They offer unconditional love, and their mere presence in the program can help provide a sense of security in children. Having an ever-present pet, for example, can help ease separation anxiety in children when Mom and Dad leave for the day. Studies have also shown that pets can help calm hyperactive or overly aggressive children. A fish tank at the child's level can have a calming and quieting effect. Not only does it provide a calming visual effect, but many large fish tanks have filters that provide a calming auditory effect.

If you decide to house a pet in your program, consider a few guidelines:
- Designate one responsible adult as the pet's caretaker.
- Be aware that pets will likely get too much attention from children and not enough from adults.
- Clearly spell out expectations for handling the pet.
- Supervise all interactions between children and animals, while instructing children on safe behavior when in close proximity to the animal.
- Make sure that any children who are allergic to the animal do not have any contact with it.
- Before acquiring a pet, check with your center director and follow center and state guidelines. In some places, reptiles are not allowed as classroom pets because of the risk of disease.

139

Touch

Touch can convey a message of caring and understanding and is recognized as an important part of a child's development. Humans need to be cuddled and touched to be physically and emotionally healthy. Touch is an instinct, a natural response to feelings of affection, compassion, need, and joy. Children need copious amounts of positive human touch in all types: carrying, swinging, holding, backrubs, hugs, pats, high fives, and fist bumps. Caring touch from adults is critical for children to feel nurtured and secure, and interactions with their peers help develop social and emotional competence.

GUIDELINES FOR USING TOUCH THERAPY

Even with all the benefits of touch, educators need to be cautious. The stories in the media and sensationalized court cases have made many teachers uneasy about touching children. Know your center's policies regarding touch, and know your students well enough to have a good idea of how they will respond.

- Respect the feelings and needs of individuals. Some people are afraid to touch because of cultural conditioning, emotional deprivation, physical trauma, or abuse.
- An adult must ask permission before touching a child.
- Be sure that the touch never gives a mixed message. Touch is always nonsexual and never passionate. Touch should always be compassionate.
- Written policies regarding physical touch require clear understanding among all staff and need to be fully communicated to children, families, and caregivers.

Touch is the most powerful form of communication! Through touch, you can communicate messages of safety, security, trust, self-worth, belonging, appreciation, happiness, and caring to children.

AFFIRMATIONS

Children can be bombarded with negative comments and criticism by adults. This has a tremendous effect on their self-concept. To counteract the effects of negative criticism that children may be experiencing, educators can provide affirmations. Affirmations communicate attention, acceptance, and approval to the child. Since children innately want to please adults, one of the most powerful techniques for eliciting appropriate behavior is to notice and comment positively when a child engages in a desired behavior. Affirmations can play a powerful role in developing prosocial behavior and self-efficacy.

CHILDREN'S BOOKS

Reading to children is a very important component to their development. Children's literature provides a safe medium for children to explore concepts, feelings, and attitudes and allows them to better understand their environment, community, and societal expectations. In her book *Books to Grow With: A Guide to Using the Best Children's Fiction for Everyday Issues and Tough Challenges,* Cheryl Coon asserts that reading to children increases self-esteem, gives comfort, and may help children cope with difficult situations. Children's literature is an engaging way to introduce new concepts and vocabulary and to stimulate meaningful conversations. Discussing the various characters and how they respond to their emotions can be a very helpful exercise. It also helps to refer to the characters when similar feelings arise in the child. This type of quick reminder can be a useful trigger to help the child transition from a purely emotional reaction to one that brings more positive results.

When children experience difficulties in their daily lives, reading about characters with similar problems helps them cope. Narratives outside the child's individual situation provide story lines that aid in understanding

their own feelings and help children realize they are not alone in their situation. With a correctly chosen book, story characters provide examples to guide the child through distress or challenges. The power of using children's books as a creative strategy lies in the fact that children can learn from and be comforted by the challenges of fictional characters in a way that feels safely separate from—yet deeply relevant to—their own lives.

In one study, researchers explored the use of children's books as a successful intervention strategy with children who are dealing with bullying. They found that through the use of books, children began to communicate their own experiences with bullying and were able to develop coping strategies to deal with teasing and harassment (Coon, 2004)

Books also provide a basis for communication between two individuals, which is particularly helpful when dealing with difficult subject matter. Children's books are often used to open lines of communication among children, families, and teachers.

Coon suggests that reading and discussing books that focus on a specific topic is a wonderful way to present positive models to children. When using children's books as a creative strategy, consider the following goals:
- to provide information
- to provide insight
- to stimulate discussions
- to communicate new values and attitudes
- to create the awareness that others have dealt with similar problems
- to become aware of feelings
- to develop empathetic responses

Finding the right book at the right time to address a challenging behavior can be surprisingly easy. Books cover a variety of topics from bedwetting to bullying and peer pressure to sibling rivalry. Your first and best resource is a good librarian, who often will know exactly what to recommend. At the very least, he will be able to assist you in researching various options. There are also a number of books and websites that offer lists of recommended reading pertaining to specific issues. (See Web Resources, page 204.)

When developing your library or book center, include books that address common stressful situations, such as disagreement among peers, developing independence, or losing a favorite item or toy. Also include books on more sensitive topics such as sibling rivalry, adoption,

foster homes, divorce, and single-parent families. Below is my list of recommended books for use with children.

Feelings

Feelings by Aliki. 1984. New York: William Morrow.

Today I Feel Silly: And Other Moods that Make My Day by Jamie Lee Curtis. 1998. New York: HarperCollins.

Mr. Happy by Roger Hargreaves. 1971. New York: Price Stern Sloan.

My Many Colored Days by Dr. Seuss. 1998. New York: Alfred A. Knopf.

Anger

Mean Soup by Betsy Everitt. 1992. Orlando: Harcourt Brace.

Alexander and the Terrible, Horrible, No Good, Very Bad Day by Judith Viorst. 1972. New York: Atheneum Books for Young Readers.

Anxiety

Wemberly Worried by Kevin Henkes. 2000. New York: HarperCollins.

Self-Esteem

Incredible Me! by Kathi Appelt. 2003. New York: Harper Childrens.

ABC: I Like Me! by Nancy Carlson. 1999. New York: Puffin.

I'm Gonna Like Me: Letting Off a Little Self-Esteem by Jamie Lee Curtis. 2002. New York: HarperCollins.

Chrysanthemum by Kevin Henkes. 2007. New York: HarperCollins.

Tacky the Penguin by Helen Lester. 1988. New York: Houghton Mifflin.

Because Brian Hugged His Mother by David Rice. 1999. Nevada City, CA: Dawn Publications.

Eggbert, the Slightly Cracked Egg by Tom Ross. 1997. New York: Puffin.

The Sneetches and Other Stories by Dr. Seuss. 1961. New York: Random House.

Self-Control

Hands Are Not for Hitting by Martine Agassi. 2000. Minneapolis, MN: Free Spirit.

Separation

The Kissing Hand by Audrey Penn. 1993. Terre Haute, IN: Tanglewood.

I Miss You Every Day by Simms Taback. 2007. New York: Viking.

Manners

Monster Manners by Bethany Roberts. 1996. New York: Clarion.

Friendship

Charlie the Caterpillar by Dom DeLuise. 1990. New York: Aladdin.

Horace and Morris but Mostly Dolores by James Howe. 2003. Pine Plains, NY: Live Oak Media.

Enemy Pie by Derek Munson. 2000. San Franciso: Chronicle.

Listening Skills

Listen Buddy by Helen Lester. 1995. New York: Houghton Mifflin.

Empathy

Hey, Little Ant by Phillip Hoose and Hannah Hoose. 1998. Berkeley, CA: Tricycle Press.

Divorce

I Don't Want to Talk about It by Jeanie Franz Ransom. 2000. Washington, DC: Magination Press.

Death

The Dead Bird by Margaret Wise Brown. 1995. New York: HarperCollins.

CHOOSING A CHILDREN'S BOOK AS A CREATIVE STRATEGY

When choosing children books as a creative strategy, consider the following points:

- Can children identify with the plot, setting, dialogue, and characters?
- Does the book use correct terminology and psychologically sound explanations?
- Does the book portray events accurately?
- Are the origins of emotional reactions revealed and inspected?
- Does the book reflect an appreciation for individual differences?
- Are good coping strategies modeled for the child?
- Does the book present conflict in an optimistic and surmountable fashion?
- Does the book have professional endorsements?

The value of children's books is not contingent upon reading or discussion. There are other ways to explore and follow up on reading experiences, such as drawing, journaling, composing alternate endings or sequels, dramatic play, and storytelling.

One unique creative strategy is to develop your own classroom or individual book. These personalized books can be created by an adult on topics associated with challenging behaviors that may be relevant to the class or a particular child. Consider creating a book for a child that helps her understand social interactions, situations, expectations, and social cues or rules. It can identify a concern and develop a script that supports the desired outcome. When children receive information that helps them understand the expectations of a situation, their challenging behavior within that situation often is reduced or minimized.

DRAMATIC PLAY

In dramatic play, children pretend and take on the roles and interactions of those they observe in their environment. As they interact with their peers in dramatic play, children learn how to appropriately interrelate and engage in various environments and situations. They have the opportunity to practice successful social interactions, which sets them up for achievement both in and out of the classroom.

Research shows that children who engage in dramatic play tend to demonstrate more empathy toward others, because they have experienced pretending to be someone else for a while. They have the skills to cooperate with peers, control impulses, and are less aggressive than children who do not engage in this type of play. Through dramatic play, children can take on a role, as well as the feelings and emotions associated with it. They have a forum to relate to others, practicing relationships they may actually carry out later in life.

Dramatic play in the preschool setting provides children with many developmental advantages necessary to later success in school. One of these advantages, self-regulation, has a strong correlation to academic and social success for children. Without quality self-regulation skills, children are at a disadvantage, unable to effectively learn new information and maintain appropriate relationships with their peers. During dramatic play, children learn social skills and how to manage their emotions, because children create the rules. Children also keep track of who follows the rules and how the play is facilitated.

Dramatic play is an essential period of the day in preschool. The teacher holds a direct role in how dramatic playtime is run, what props are used, and what materials are available. The teacher not only is responsible for the setup and organization of dramatic play but also for the structure and quality of the playtime. The teacher must find a balance in intervention, giving support to his students to enhance the benefits of dramatic play, but not becoming too involved or interfering with the spontaneity and child-directed nature of it.

In addition to benefits for all children in the program, dramatic play can be tremendous fun for the individual child and can be mutually gratifying for both the child and the adult. Dramatic play provides an opportunity for the adult to present positive models of psychological constructs, including thought, feeling, and behavior, in an unobtrusive and informal manner. Through dramatic play, you also have the opportunity to model positive behaviors and to observe any trouble spots in the child's behavior that need guidance or intervention, such as bossiness or a reluctance to clean up.

Most of the dramatic play centers in early childhood classrooms are set up like a house; in many cases, the setting is just a kitchen area. Some of these house-themed dramatic play centers include dress-up clothes, dolls, and miniature furniture. And although such setups are a great start to the dramatic play center, find ways to introduce variety. Children need rich and diverse experiences over time to learn and develop. Change the dramatic play center regularly, based on your students' interests or the themes you are teaching.

There are many possible themes and setups for a dramatic play center. The most important thing is that the environment is safe, with appropriate assorted materials that students can use for active and effective pretend play.

One of the most powerful roles adults can have in intervening with challenging behavior is to become part of the child's dramatic play, especially those roles associated with the victims of violence. Many adults are not naturally good players. Here are some helpful reminders to being a positive and effective player during dramatic play:

146

DRAMATIC PLAY AREA IDEAS

Airplane	Castle	Iceberg	Post office
Airport	Cave	Ice-cream shop	Rain forest
Animal shelter	Circus	Igloo	Ranch
Aquarium	Construction site	Jewelry store	Ranger station
Art gallery	Farm	Mall	Recording studio
Bakery	Fire station	Medical supply store	Research lab
Barnyard	Florist	Movie theater	Restaurant
Beach	Garage	Museum	Radio station
Beauty shop	Garden	Nursery	Safari
Bookstore	Grocery store	Office	Sailboat
Bus station	Hair salon	Pet store	Shoe repair
Campground	Haunted house	Pizza parlor	Space station
Candy shop	Health club	Planetarium	Submarine
Car wash	Hospital	Police station	TV station

- Play the part of someone other than yourself.
- If you are familiar with the plot of the story, make up a new one when there is a lull in the action.
- Be careful not to be too directive or active, such as overpowering the children with your own themes or telling the children's characters what to do.
- Have your characters show excitement over positive anticipation; show intense involvement or pleasure in solving a problem that comes up.
- Keep in mind a number of basic, nonviolent themes.

What should you do when the child's dramatic play focuses on violent themes? (The plot of almost all action/adventure violent themes is that the persecutor pursues the victim and a rescuer disables the persecutor.) Wait quietly until the violent episode is over, to avoid reinforcing it. Then, have a character who is a friend of the victim be very concerned about the victim, sad that he was hurt, and nurturing the victim if he is still alive or supportive of the relatives if he is dead. Model the friends of the victim grieving and problem solving in an appropriate manner.

PUPPETS

Puppets are a wonderful tool to address challenging behavior in the preschool classroom. It does not really matter what kind of puppet you use—in fact, you can just talk with your hand, and children will pay attention and find it funny. Have you ever watched a live puppet show? Something about having a puppet talking to you draws you in. Puppets foster social interaction, communication, role playing, imagination, storytelling, listening, and much more. Do not think your students are too old or too young for puppets; people of all ages are intrigued by puppets. Puppets can be used in the program to help children express their feelings and understand social situations in a relevant yet entertaining manner.

Using puppets to talk with children about their problems is a valuable tool to foster communication about situations that affect their behavior. Puppets allow children to think about solutions to conflicts; by role playing with puppets, children can improve their ability to experience empathy, the understanding of what others might be thinking. Children who talk about different points of view with props such as puppets often have an easier time getting along with others and developing friendships.

Puppets also can introduce feeling words, such as *sad, mad,* and *frustrated.* By bringing puppets into the group time, adults can create a strong sense of community in their program.

Here are some basic tips for using puppets with young children:

■ Try out each puppet before buying it, keeping your students in mind. Does your hand fit well inside the puppet? Is your puppet friendly looking? Look for faces that can change to show expressions and hands or paws that move.

■ Select diverse puppets with care. Include a range of cultures, abilities, and backgrounds. Consider using animals, too.

■ Think about your puppet's personality. Is he fearful, feisty, or flexible? A range of puppets gives every child "someone like me."

Pointers for performing with puppets:

■ If this is your initial experience with puppets, it may be helpful to write a script. Even if you do not use the script, it will help you remember what you want to say.

149

- Use different voices for puppets. Change the rhythm and intonation of the voice pattern for each puppet.
- Use childlike language. Your puppet will seem more like a real child if it uses words and sentences similar to those children use.
- Invite staff members and parents who speak another language to become puppeteers. Then your puppets can model dual language use and teach the children to try out new words in that language.
- Make sure each puppet has a range of experiences and behaviors. This way, children will not label puppets "bad" or "good." Everyone has problems and successes.
- Use real toys as props when acting out conflicts over things. For example, use real manipulatives if puppets are fighting over them.

Following are potential activities for using puppets to address challenging behaviors. Countless scenarios can be played out to provide teachable moments focusing on natural consequences, feelings, and resolving conflicts.

- Have a puppet pretend to bite another puppet or even the adult. Use the scenario as a teachable moment by discussing the natural consequences of biting, especially how the victim feels and the pain biting may cause.
- Have the puppets cheer each other up when someone is feeling sad.
- Arrange the puppets in a seated semicircle, and pretend one of them is a student who invades others' personal space and has a difficult time remaining in his designated area.
- Whisper to one of the puppets to chase one of the children. Have the puppet look at the child, then look back at you, pausing dramatically before chasing.
- Have the puppet experience difficulty going to sleep during nap time. Instead of sleeping, have the puppet make noises and continually get off its cot to wander around.
- Have one of the smaller puppets shake and be afraid of one of the larger ones. Have the smaller one stand up for itself to the larger one.

MUSIC

Music is deeply rooted in human cultures. Without it, life would not be the same. Take a moment and imagine if you had never heard classic children's songs such as "Twinkle, Twinkle, Little Star," "The Itsy Bitsy Spider," or the "ABC Song." It's unthinkable. Experiences with music start in early childhood and last a lifetime.

Music is an incredibly powerful form of expression, combining both words and sound to deliver a message. Hearing certain songs on the radio can trigger very specific memories. Music is highly motivating, yet it also can have a calming and relaxing effect. Enjoyable music activities can help children feel better about themselves and can have significant effects on children's overall well-being that last well into adulthood. Research proves the value of introducing children to music while they are very young.

Music plays a key role in creating an enriching, stimulating environment for children. Children have a natural love for music—they really enjoy a good tune with an energetic beat. A powerful stimulant, music can alter a child's mood instantly and can help create new bonds and memories. Simply listening to music is enjoyable and fun, but extensive research has shown that exposing children to music actually stimulates their overall intelligence and emotional development. Having children listen to different types of music can help nurture their self-esteem by encouraging creativity, self-confidence, and curiosity. Music helps children synthesize experiences, transition into new activities, calm down during nap time, and build a sense of community.

Choi, Lee, and Lee have found that involvement in music activities from an early age helps children develop good social and emotional skills. Psychologists, neuroscientists, and experts in early childhood development have demonstrated that music does even more than that: it helps children's brain cells make the connections needed for virtually every kind of intelligence. In particular, when children are consistently engaged by music in an age-appropriate, socially accepting environment, they benefit from the ability to regulate their responses and relate to others in complex ways.

Many researchers believe that the earlier a child is exposed to music, the more her brain responds to different musical tones. We know that children are easily able to imitate musical phrases and songs. As toddlers, they love to bang on pots and pans, searching for that certain beat they play over and over again—it is their way of expressing emotions. As they get older, they sing, improvise, move, and dance and are often introduced to instruments and formal music instruction.

Brain researchers note that music activates neural systems of reward and emotion similar to those stimulated by food and sex. Music "tickles" the brain in a highly pleasurable way—it releases endorphins that provide

151

feelings of happiness and energy. Children welcome tools to better handle their relationships and emotions and to practice positive thinking.

Many people believe that music can heal the soul, but can it help cure physical and mental ailments? Richard Edwards and Donald Hodges reviewed studies on the effects of music on patients with cancer, attention deficit disorder, and depression. Research has shown that music is effective in helping people cope, both mentally and physically. Some hospitals use music to help patients manage their illnesses because music calms the mind and eases stress. Gwendolyn Watkins found that music can stimulate the production of endorphins, the body's natural opiates, as well as reduce levels of cortisol and noradrenaline, hormones related to stress. It has been observed that specific tones, notes, or pitches have a powerful effect on the body, which can help a patient restore and improve emotional, psychological, and physiological health.

Numerous research studies have documented the positive effects music can have:
- reduced muscle tension
- improved self-image
- increased self-esteem
- decreased anxiety and agitation
- increased verbalization
- enhanced interpersonal relationships
- improved group cohesiveness
- increased motivation
- successful and safe emotional release

In addition, Glenn Schellenberg has found that music can contribute to an increase in overall intelligence by shaping the attitudes, interests, and discipline within children. Many types of music can be inspiring and incredibly motivational, thereby helping children focus and improving their listening skills. Music can help children attain the self-confidence and self-esteem they need to succeed and define personality traits as they grow older. Shannon Sausser and Raymond Waller discovered a wide variety of examples where music helped increase self-confidence and self-esteem. Ae-Na Choi, Myeong Soo Lee, and Jung-Sook Lee found that music can reduce aggressive behavior and improve self-esteem in children with highly aggressive behavior. Deborah Bradway found that having children participate in music not only promotes development of self-esteem through successful educational and social interactions, but also enables children to use the group as a support system, as a replacement for what may be lacking in family structure and rituals.

There are many fun and inexpensive ways for you to explore music with children. Here are some interesting ideas to try:

- **Sing:** You may not be the next singing sensation, but children will not notice if you cannot carry a tune, and you will have a lot of fun together.
- **Make music:** Get creative and look for everyday things you can transform into musical instruments; for example, make maracas out of plastic bottles by simply filling them with some small pebbles and sealing the top.
- **Explore many types of music:** Add variety by playing a different type of music each day—classical, country, rock, rap, big band, jazz, oldies, camp songs, or simply old-fashioned children's music.
- **Buy inexpensive instruments:** The harmonica, recorder, and kazoo are inexpensive ways to introduce children to instruments and to have them experiment with creating different sounds and tunes. Provide several of each instrument, and be sure to sterilize the instruments after each use.
- **Create songs:** Focus on positive behaviors and social skills as you create new song lyrics using familiar melodies such as "Twinkle, Twinkle, Little Star" or "Mary Had a Little Lamb." You can personalize the songs for your classroom and for individual children.

153

- **Enroll in a workshop:** There are so many workshops available, and some of them are surprisingly affordable. Expand your knowledge of music by choosing one that offers a good variety of activities, such as making music with different instruments or using music play and movement in the classroom.
- **Encourage performance:** Children love to perform. Put on a favorite CD or a song from your playlist and encourage the children to dance, sing, and enjoy themselves.
- **Play songs as background music:** Play songs from a CD or playlist while the children engage in other activities. As the children interact in the centers, they will listen and sing the melodies to themselves, working these songs into their schemas.
- **Personalize music:** Children's songs that have been customized to include a child's name can bring hours of fun and enjoyment to your program. Just imagine the look of surprise and wonder when the children hear their names being sung in their favorite songs. Personalized CDs can spark creativity and boost self-confidence in children, making them feel very special.
- **Understand and label emotions:** Singing specific songs about feelings, skills, and behaviors helps children with expectations for certain situations. Listed below are a number of songs for children that accomplish this goal:

"Be the Kind of Person," *Like a Star*, Jim Rule

"Body Check," *Tuned Into Learning, Volume 1: Social Skills and Pragmatics for Autism and Related Needs*

"Body Talk," *Tuned Into Learning, Volume 1: Social Skills and Pragmatics for Autism and Related Needs*

"Compliments," *Tuned Into Learning, Volume 1: Social Skills and Pragmatics for Autism and Related Needs*

"Count to Ten!" *Like a Star*, Jim Rule

"Don't Be Bossy," *Songs to Get Along*, Todd Werner

"Eye to Eye," *Exploring Language through Song and Play*, Captain Al

"Hands to Yourself," *Getting Better at Getting Along*, Jack Hartmann

"Hello 'Round the World," *Sing Me Your Story*, Two of a Kind

"I Can Problem Solve," *Character Counts*, Todd Werner

"I Can Say 'No' When I Want To," *Caring and Capable Kids*, Linda K. Williams and Susanna Palomares

"I'm Sorry," *Like a Star*, Jim Rule

"Jumping to Conclusions," *Everyone's Invited*, Vitamin L

"No One Is a Nobody," *Caring and Capable Kids*, Linda K. Williams and Susanna Palomares

154

"Look at Your Neighbor," *Tuned Into Learning, Volume 1: Social Skills and Pragmatics for Autism and Related Needs*

"Show Kindness Every Day," *Lullabies and Quiet-Time Songs for Children*, Jack Hartmann

"Strategy Wheel," *Come Join the Circle: Lesson Songs for Peacemaking*, Paulette Meier

"Taking Turns," *Exploring Language through Song and Play*, Captain Al

"Talking 'Bout a Put-Down," *Everyone's Invited*, Vitamin L

"This Is the Way," *Getting Better at Getting Along*, Jack Hartmann

"T.I.M.E. at the Peace Table," *Come Join the Circle: Lesson Songs for Peacemaking*, Paulette Meier

"We All Have Feelings," *Mixing It Up!* Margie La Bella

"What Does Peace Mean?" *Come Join the Circle: Lesson Songs for Peacemaking*, Paulette Meier

"What Should I Do?" *Caring and Capable Kids*, Linda K. Williams and Susanna Palomares

"Who I Am Makes a Difference," *Caring and Capable Kids*, Linda K. Williams and Susanna Palomares

"Work It Out with Words," *Getting Better at Getting Along*, Jack Hartmann

Music plays a powerful role in the lives of children. Through music, children can better understand themselves and their feelings, learn to decipher patterns, solve problems, and discover the world around them in rich, complex ways.

CREATIVE EXPRESSION

Abraham Maslow and Sigmund Freud considered creative expression to be a fundamental biological need—one that defines our existence and the human condition. Creative expression enhances healthy personalities and is a way to communicate feelings and thoughts that otherwise may be difficult to express. Creative expression enhances children's cognitive processes, involving them in problem solving, thinking, and using symbol systems to record their thoughts, ideas, and feelings.

Creative expression is a natural form of communication for children because it is easier for them to express themselves visually than verbally. In her book *The Joyful Child: A Sourcebook of Activities and Ideas for Releasing Children's Natural Joy*, Peggy Jenkins points out that creative expression enhances cognitive abilities, improves social skills, and encourages self-esteem in children. In addition, it helps children manage stress and build empathy with peers and provides a safe place to express, release, and work through emotions.

Children's creative expression is a language, a highly symbolic activity that requires the child to think of an experience, idea, or feeling and then find symbols to express it. If children do not feel secure, safe, and comfortable with themselves, they will not be able to take the risk or meet the challenges involved in producing art. Thus, it is extremely important to accept and respect any creative expressions by children.

As they engage in the creative process, children learn they can observe, organize, and interpret their experiences. They can make decisions, take actions, and monitor the effects of those actions. They can create form and meaning where none existed before. The artistic experience becomes a source of communication and interaction between children and adults.

Children feel a sense of emotional satisfaction when they are involved in creative expression, whether they are modeling with clay, drawing with crayons, or making a collage from recycled scraps. This satisfaction comes from the control children have over the materials they use and the autonomy they have in the decisions they make. Deciding what they will make and which materials to use might be the first opportunity children have to make independent choices and decisions.

Creative expression builds children's self-esteem. When children participate in creative activities with classmates, the feedback they give each other builds self-esteem by helping them learn to accept criticism and acknowledgement from others. Small group art activities also help children practice important social skills such as taking turns, sharing, and negotiating for materials.

Respect for children's creative expressions means giving them time to grow, explore, and experiment with materials. Children should not be hurried or pressured into representing their ideas or feelings through creative expressions, nor to be interested in the product (much less to produce one). Children who have had the opportunity to explore and experiment with materials as toddlers are more ready as preschoolers and primary students to find out how they can gain control over and use the materials to express themselves. Children will not be bored using the same media over and over. As long as they have something new and

156

exciting to say, children will find new and different ways to use the same paints, clay, crayons, paper, and markers to give form to their ideas.

Early childhood educators can be neutral observers during the creative process or can engage in a richer role by talking with the children about their expressions. This interaction will enable children to expand on and share their unique perspectives of their world. In creative expression, the focus must be on the process. Creative expression enables the children to be involved in what the process has to offer rather than how their products will be evaluated.

The creative process has four characteristics: fluency, flexibility, originality, and elaboration. Fluency refers to the purposeful interaction among the material, the child's body, and his ideas. The flexibility of creative expression gives children the freedom to experiment in their own ways with different approaches to the materials. Creative expression allows children to demonstrate originality by deciding what to make and how to make it. They can elaborate on their creations by adding new materials or details to their expressions.

Early childhood professionals can encourage the creative process in a number of ways:

- Allow children to enjoy the freedom that basic materials provide.
- Let the children select topics and subjects that are important to them.
- Give them time to explore relationships among materials.
- Give them the opportunity to arrange materials into their own creations.
- Let them stay with what they are doing until they say it is done.
- Give them the chance to express their feelings, thoughts, and ideas in a creative manner.
- Nurture their creativity when responding to their expressions.

Aromatherapy

Aromatherapy can give comfort and peace, which is why it has been used since ancient times and remains popular today. Use aromatherapy to create a relaxing environment, decrease the stress and tension of daily life, stimulate imagination and creativity, and promote concentration. Certain smells boost, relax, warm, or cheer us. They can trigger memories, increase focus, and stimulate appetite. Think of warm bread straight out

of the oven or freshly ground coffee. Imagine the scent of a sun-kissed rose. Close your eyes and smell freshly crushed mint, a field of wild thyme, wood smoke, lemon zest, hot chocolate, or cut grass.

Children learn best through play, and it is easy to find playful ways to teach children about the power of scent. A nature walk is the perfect time to talk about all of the smells you encounter. Take note of the scents your students enjoy—these are great clues for knowing what they might like to smell more of in the program.

Include scents in the classroom by making or buying items that bring smells to playtime. With a little thoughtfulness and imagination, scent can be added to nearly any topic or item. Scented playdough is very popular, and you can develop fine-motor-skill play boxes using containers that have lingering smells, such as cocoa boxes or tea tins.

In her book *Aromatherapy: A Holistic Guide,* Ann Berwick defines aromatherapy as the therapeutic use of the essential oils of aromatic plants. Essential oils are highly concentrated, volatile extracts distilled

WHEN NOTHING ELSE WORKS

from aromatic herbs, flowers, and trees. Many contain hormone-like properties and are natural antiseptics.

Safety note: Do not ingest essential oils or put essential oils on the skin. Keep all essential oils out of the reach of children. Essential oils can cause problems in people who have asthma, allergies, or sensitivity to odor. Be sure to follow your center and state guidelines for using these materials with young children, who can be particularly sensitive to essential oils.

To understand how essential oils can affect an individual's emotional state, we need to understand some of the physical properties involved. Only three inches separate the olfactory receptor sites and the brain—the nerve fibers of the olfactory system run directly to the limbic area of the brain, which contains areas linked to the perception of odor, pleasure and pain, emotions, and sexual feelings. Olfactory messages also do not pass through the spinal cord, as most other nerve messages in the body do. Finally, the olfactory system is one of the paths we can use to bypass the blood-brain barrier. This is extremely important therapeutically and shows why we can influence moods and emotions so quickly and effectively through scent.

Lavender, for example, is one of the most widely used of all aromatherapy oils. It appears to have a calming and soothing effect on children and adults.

Warning: Do not apply products that contain lavender oil topically; ONLY use them for aromatherapy. Lavender might not be safe for children, especially young boys who have not yet reached puberty. Lavender oil seems to have hormone effects that could disrupt the normal hormones in a boy's body. In some cases, this has resulted in boys developing abnormal breast growth. The safety of these products when used by young girls is not known.

The easiest and most effective method of dispersing essential oil into the environment is through the air. This can easily be done by using a new plant sprayer. Fill the bottle with one cup of warm (not boiling) water, add two drops of essential oil, and gently shake. The water dilutes the oil so that it is not toxic. This mixture can be sprayed into the air or on carpets, curtains, or furniture, but do not let the water fall on wood.

CHAPTER 8 ■ CREATIVE STRATEGIES TO TRY WHEN NOTHING ELSE WORKS

WHEN NOTHING ELSE WORKS

9

ACKNOWLEDGING BEHAVIOR

As early childhood educators, we want children in our programs to have positive behaviors. Acknowledgment systems can effectively increase prosocial behavior, focus staff and children's attention on desired behaviors, and foster a positive climate. Once children have been introduced to the expectations of the preschool program, they need acknowledgment for demonstrating the expected behaviors. Acknowledgment helps promote and maintain these desired behaviors.

It is empowering to know you can change the climate in your program simply by focusing on the positive behaviors of children. Using this simple strategy, teachers can devote more time and attention to desirable behaviors than they do to challenging behaviors.

It is a win-win situation: teachers want children to exhibit positive behaviors and children want their teacher's approval. The old adage, "You catch more flies with honey than with vinegar," is certainly true when guiding children.

Acknowledgement systems can be used with children of all ages, from toddlers to high school students, with typically developing children, and with children who have special needs, such as emotional, physical, communication or cognitive concerns.

Children constantly seek attention from the adults who care for them. The need for adult attention is so great that children will settle for negative attention. Your reactions to a child's behavior help determine future behavior; for example, if you snicker when a child says an obscene word, she is likely to keep saying it. It stands to reason, then, that paying attention to challenging behavior can actually result in an increase in this type of conduct. On the other hand, acknowledging children's positive behaviors can lead to increases in social skills, playing well with other children, and following adult directions and can lead to decreases in such behaviors as aggressiveness and destructiveness. When adults focus on positive behaviors, they spend less precious time responding to challenging behaviors and do not need to use correction as often to control behaviors. Most importantly, the overall climate of the program is significantly more positive, thus developing a community of caring individuals.

This acknowledgment strategy primarily is based on three findings by Matthew Timm and Sharon Doubet that involved children and the adults who supported them.

First, a child's behavior will increase or decrease depending on what immediately happens after the behavior is exhibited. For example, if a child says a curse word and adults immediately start laughing, there is a high probability that the child will continue to use that obscene word.

Secondly, adults tend to focus more on negative behaviors than they do positive ones, which reduces the likelihood of recognizing and encouraging prosocial behavior when it occurs.

Finally, even if we intervene with challenging behavior, we cannot assume that the behavior will not occur again. A child must develop a positive alternative to the disruptive behavior that helps him obtain the desire or the need. For example, if a child is not able to remain in his assigned area during group time and you remove him from the group as a consequence, it does not mean that he will know how to sit on his carpet square when he returns to the group experience. The positive behavior needs to be discussed, modeled, practiced, and encouraged to continue.

TYPES OF ACKNOWLEDGEMENT SYSTEMS

The most effective acknowledgment systems contain both formal and informal components. Formal acknowledgements include reinforcers such as focusing on tangible items, social recognition, or preferred activities to promote positive behavior. Informal acknowledgments are positive descriptive statements and nonverbal recognition, such as a smile.

INFORMAL ACKNOWLEGEMENTS

There are many ways to acknowledge prosocial behaviors informally: tell children you are proud of their efforts, or give them a high five, thumbs-up, or hug. Informal acknowledgments such as these are critical for establishing a positive classroom environment.

When using verbal acknowledgement to increase the likelihood that positive behaviors will continue, consider the following guidelines:

- **Be descriptive:** Rather than just saying "great job" or "thanks," provide a brief description of the behavior you observed. For example, "Michael, thank you for helping Alex put the blocks away." This feedback helps children know exactly which behaviors you would like to see again.
- **Be enthusiastic**: Metacommunication such as tone of voice, facial expressions, and personal space affect the spirit in which positive statements are accepted. Your enthusiasm when you deliver feedback conveys to children that you are paying attention to them, that their behavior matters to you, and that you celebrate their accomplishments and effort.
- **Recognize effort:** Children need to be encouraged for their efforts as well as their successes. Know each child well enough to be able to recognize small accomplishments and individualize your responses— for example, "Jimmy, you were able to remain on your carpet square for the first page of the story."

163

- **Be positive:** Positive Behavior Support programs promote a ratio of five positive statements for every correction. Cognitive behaviorists such as Maxwell Maltz recommend a ratio of 12 positives to one negative statement. From the neuroscience perspective, positive behavior must continue for 21 days in a row, without ever displaying the negative behavior during that time period, to develop a neural circuit within the brain. In real-life terms, that means that if one of your students hits another child to obtain an item, and you want him to use words to express his needs instead of hitting, the prosocial behavior needs to occur 21 days in a row to develop that permanent neural circuit in the brain. If the child regresses and exhibits the hitting behavior, the 21-day period begins again from scratch. Negative behavior is not impossible to change, but based on this premise, it is difficult to alter. Please do not give up hope! For some of your most vulnerable children, your hope may be all that they have.

When you notice a behavior that you want to see the child continue, use nonverbal acknowledgement (a smile, a wink, a thumbs-up, or a high five) to let the child know that you notice and welcome the behavior. Nonverbal acknowledgements can be sent and received across the room, hallway, or playground. Research shows that the average child returns 60 to 80 percent of smiles; so, a genuine smile can make a real difference in your program. The difficult part is consistently implementing those nonverbal acknowledgements for each child and every positive behavior you want to recognize.

There are many ways to provide positive responses and express your approval. By being mindful and putting this approach into practice, you will find yourself being far more positive in your interactions with students. In addition to these informal efforts, consider having formal systems for acknowledging students' positive behaviors.

FORMAL ACKNOWLEGEMENTS

Formal systems clearly specify desired behaviors and involve acknowledging these behaviors with predefined rewards. Formal systems can either be in place all the time or only at certain times. There is an ongoing debate in early childhood literature about the appropriateness of using rewards with young children. Some prominent early childhood educators such as Alfie Kohn criticize teachers' reliance on rewards to obtain children's participation in otherwise uninteresting activities.

WHEN NOTHING ELSE WORKS

Kohn has been the most articulate voice opposing the use of rewards in educational settings, arguing that rewards lead to children feeling controlled and that they undermine children's intrinsic motivation to learn and achieve. He asserts that his views are supported by the findings of numerous research studies showing that rewards are strikingly ineffective at producing lasting changes in attitudes or behaviors.

I agree that teachers should provide classroom experiences that engage children's interest and desire to learn and should try to refrain from using formal systems to internally motivate children to learn. However, when dealing with challenging behavior, research has shown that formal systems can assist children who have difficulty with sensory processing, following basic expectations for behavior, learning guidelines for social interaction, or controlling impulsive behaviors. Formal systems can help these children succeed in early childhood programs.

As more children with challenging behavior enter early childhood programs, teachers can consider formal systems as an alternative, instead of insisting their programs cannot adapt and meet these children's unique needs.

Table 9.1

EXAMPLES OF SPECIFIC REWARDS FOR CHILDREN

Preferred Activities	Social Recogntion	Tangibles
Line leader	Recognition certificate	Stickers
Lunch helper	Call home to parents	Hand stamps
Pick book to read	Note home to parents	Small toys
Extra time in a center	Recognition at circle time	Crayons or markers
Sit near friend	Picture on board	Temporary tattoo
First on the tricycle	Holding a special item	Smelling box
Choice of activity	Recognition necklace	Feeling box
Sitting next to teacher	Recognition pin	Unbreakable mirror

Take into consideration the developmental level of the students as you create the formal acknowledgement system. Determine the type and frequency of rewards that will be provided to students and consider including the children in the process of determining what rewards will be available. Regardless of the rewards chosen, the system must be easy and efficient to use.

Formal systems can be carried out in a way that includes children as proud participants and can reduce the discouraging feedback for negative behaviors. The children will feel empowered rather than minimized, neglected, or controlled.

IMPLEMENTING ACKNOWLEDGEMENT

The children in your class will develop best when you build nurturing and responsive relationships with them. Acknowledging positive behavior is an easy way to bolster those relationships. Children's behaviors and the feel of your classroom environment will change when you give positive responses to prosocial behaviors and ignore challenging behaviors. Your children want your attention and approval. Give it to them when they exhibit positive behaviors and those behaviors will continue.

You cannot—and should not—ignore behavior that is harmful to the child or others, or that destroys property.

Many educators worry that their programs will go completely out of control if they do not respond to challenging behaviors. When you initially ignore a behavior, the behavior most likely will increase in intensity and frequency as a way to "test" you. However, if you respond to positive behaviors in conjunction with ignoring negative behaviors, you will see improvement.

An acknowledgement plan in the early childhood program typically involves four steps:

1. Decide on the targeted desirable behavior that you realistically think the child can master, such as remaining on her carpet square during story time.
2. Define the behavior that you want to see increase (remaining on the carpet square).
3. Consider where, when, and how often you will look for that behavior (large group and small group time).

WHEN NOTHING ELSE WORKS

4. Think of situations to increase the likelihood of the child engaging in that behavior.

After choosing the targeted behavior, determine which informal and formal acknowledgement systems you will employ. How will you respond when the child exhibits the desirable behavior? If the child displays the targeted behavior, will you use a preferred activity, social recognition, or a tangible item to increase the likelihood the behavior will occur again?

Once you have chosen the reward, discuss concretely with the child the goal and exactly how you will track the behavior. Consider any suggestions from the child that may lead you to adapt the rewards or make other modifications to the plan.

Implement the acknowledgement plan that you have developed, and track the desirable behaviors to determine if the acknowledgement system has increased that target behavior.

Acknowledging prosocial behaviors not only increases the chance of the child displaying these behaviors again but also maintains the behaviors in a variety of settings.

Early childhood professionals who develop acknowledgement systems are more likely to develop a proactive approach to guidance by focusing on the positive behaviors that young children exhibit instead of reacting to the array of challenging behaviors occurring in their programs. Because of their attention to the positive, they are more likely to create an atmosphere where are young children will flourish and succeed.

SPECIFIC SYSTEMS TO ACKNOWLEDGE CHILDREN'S BEHAVIOR

CHART MOVERS

Chart movers are a great way to motivate children and eliminate undesirable behavior. They work because they are interactive and fun. The child can see his progress and participate in the daily steps toward the reward. The chart stands out as a testimony of the positive behavior. To make it a fun and a rewarding experience, involve the child in creating the chart.

167

When choosing the goal on the chart, be specific with your wording. For younger children who cannot read, choose an appropriate picture and give them a detailed explanation of what you expect of them. Construct the chart so the child has a visual image of closing in on the reward.

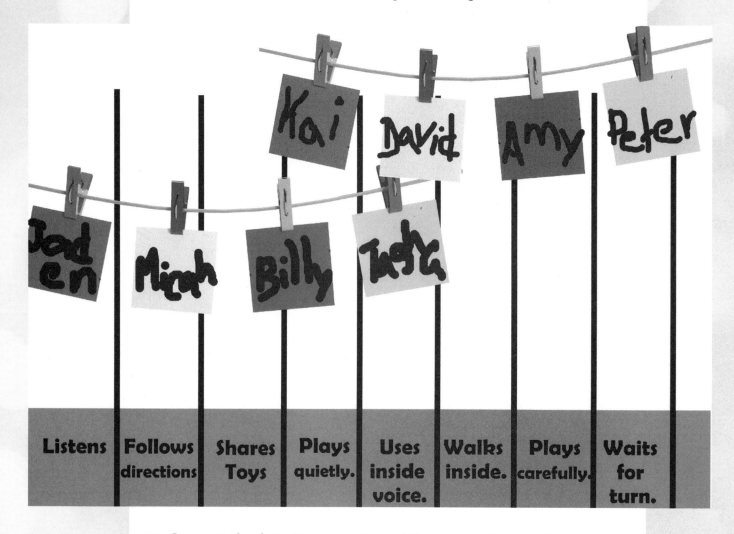

Listens | Follows directions | Shares Toys | Plays quietly. | Uses inside voice. | Walks inside. | Plays carefully. | Waits for turn.

- **Connect the dots:** Draw a picture of the reward, then outline the periphery of the picture with dots several inches apart. When the child exhibits the desired behavior, he can connect or color in the dots. When all the dots are connected or colored in, the child receives his reward.

- **Computer time:** Provide a picture of the components of a computer: monitor, console, keyboard, and mouse. As the child exhibits the desirable behavior, he earns the opportunity to color in one of the components. When all four components have been colored in, the child has the opportunity to use the classroom computer or be next in line to use it.

WHEN NOTHING ELSE WORKS

The child's developmental level will assist you in determining how many dots, steps, or bars the child must do to receive the reward; for a toddler, use end-of-the-hour rewards; for the preschooler, end-of-the-day rewards; for the school-age child, end-of-the-week rewards. A month is an unreachable eternity for any child!

MYSTERY MOTIVATOR

Mystery motivators are designed to deliver random rewards for appropriate behavior. Their use depends on you and is best suited for students who need regular motivation to demonstrate appropriate behavior or social responses. Follow these steps for effective mystery motivators:

1. Define the objective and specific behavior you want the student to increase. Clearly define the number of times you want to see the desired behavior.
2. Select some basic rewards for the student to earn with the mystery motivator. For ideas, see Table 9.1 on page 165 listing preferred activities, social recognition, and tangibles.
3. Take a picture of the selected reward, put it in a sealed envelope, and do not tell the student what it is.
4. Draw a question mark on the mystery motivator envelope, then hang the envelope in a location where it is visible to the student. It will be a constant reminder to encourage desirable behavior.
5. When the student meets the specified criteria for this behavior, immediately give her the envelope to open and receive her mystery motivator.

SUPER FRIEND ACKNOWLEDGEMENT

Introduce the concept of being a Super Friend at group time. Talk about Super Friend behaviors, which are specific, prosocial, desired behaviors. For example, a Super Friend helps his classmates clean up their area, and he shares materials or activities with his peers. Acknowledge a child's positive behaviors by presenting him with a decorated cape, vest, crown, or medallion that he can wear the rest of the day (or week). By presenting a Super Friend certificate at group time and discussing why the child is a Super Friend, you will give the children an opportunity to acknowledge each other's successes. This will motivate all children to engage in the desirable behaviors.

Spinners and Dice

Spinners and dice are a creative means to change the specific formal acknowledgment while still maintaining a high level of motivation to engage in the prosocial behavior. They keep students engaged in the process and are a fun way to deliver formal acknowledgements.

To construct the acknowledgement spinner, follow these steps:

1. Gather cardboard or card stock.
2. Cut the cardboard into a square, any size you like; 6" x 6" cardboard works well.
3. Draw a circle on the cardboard square. Alternately, you could cut out a circle to attach on top of the square.
4. Divide the circle into the desired number of sections, and label the sections with the reward for that part of the circle. The number and size of the sections depends on the type of formal acknowledgement you want to give and the chance of the student receiving that acknowledgement. For example, if the student is highly motivated to display the desired behavior for a toy car, the section representing the toy car would be rather small compared to the other preferred activities, social recognition, or additional tangible items.
5. Poke a hole in the middle of the cardboard square with scissors.
6. Cut an arrow from card stock to use as the spinner.
7. Place the arrow on the cardboard with the end of the arrow over the hole in the cardboard.
8. Poke a metal brad through the arrow into the hole in the cardboard. Spread each end of the brad open on the back side of the cardboard and tape each side down with masking tape.

The acknowledgement die is even easier to construct. Purchase or obtain a large, six-sided die. Label each side of the die with an acknowledgement: tangible, recognition, or preferred behavior. The type of formal acknowledgement and the chance of the student receiving that acknowledgement will depend on how many times the acknowledgement appears on the sides of the die. For example, if the student is highly motivated to display the desired behavior for a squishy ball, then just one side of the die would have the picture of the squishy ball. Three sides might have a picture of the child being line leader, and the last two sides might have a picture of a recognition pin. When the child exhibits the prosocial behaviors, he rolls the die to determine which formal acknowledgement he receives.

Bucket Fillers

Bucket fillers are popular in primary classrooms but easily can be adapted for early childhood programs. Carol McCloud's book *Have You Filled a Bucket Today? A Guide to Daily Happiness for Kids* suggests that we all carry an invisible bucket that contains our feelings. When our bucket is full, we feel great; when our bucket is empty, we feel sad. A bucket filler is someone who says or does nice things for other people. Of course, saying or doing something nice for someone fills the bucket filler's bucket, too.

Encourage everyone in the program, adults and children, to acknowledge and celebrate positive behaviors by using this strategy of filling each other's buckets. Provide each child with a small bucket, and let the children fill the buckets with slips of paper on which adults have written kind words or compliments dictated by the children for that specific child. Children love to watch their buckets fill with compliments.

Reducing the Rewards

As children become more adept at modeling prosocial behaviors, you can begin to reduce the frequency with which you reward the desired behavior. Magic pens are an effective means to change the schedule of reinforcement. You can purchase a set of invisible- and developer-ink pens at drug stores, office and school-supply stores, or variety stores.

On your daily schedule, use the invisible-ink pen to draw a smiley face or some other symbol inside some (not all) of the squares. After the ink dries, students should not be able to tell which squares have the invisible symbols. Explain that if a child meets the behavior expectations she has been learning, she will get to color in the square for that event with the developer pen. If the magic ink appears, the student will receive the corresponding reward immediately. For example, if you have been working with a child to encourage her to share in the block area and she is able to share during block time, you would let her color the block-time square on the schedule to see if the invisible symbol is there. If the symbol appears, she will receive a preferred activity, social recognition, or a tangible item immediately. If no ink appears, informally acknowledge the student on her behavior and tell her there might be a reward for the next event.

In the beginning, draw the invisible symbols in three-fourths of the squares, so the child has a good chance of receiving a reward. As the student's prosocial behavior occurs more frequently, reduce the number of boxes containing invisible symbols by half and then by one-fourth. Eventually, the child will no longer expect a formal acknowledgement for her prosocial behavior.

WHEN NOTHING ELSE WORKS

10

DEVELOPING AN INTERVENTION PLAN

When children continue using challenging behavior after other methods have been tried, early childhood educators and families must team together to develop an intervention plan that can be used in all environments by all team members. The plan is designed for a specific child and provides an effective approach to address concerns about persistent challenging behavior and to help the child learn to change his behavior.

First, determine the nature and function of a child's behavior. Then, the team can begin developing the intervention plan. Effective support plans consist of multiple interventions or support strategies; they are not punishment. Positive intervention plans increase the acquisition and use of new alternative skills, decrease the problem behavior, and facilitate general improvements in the quality of life for the individual and his family. As your team develops the intervention plan, keep in mind some key characteristics of individual positive behavioral support interventions:

- Focus on the whole child.
- Teach the child coping strategies.
- Be proactive and strength based.
- Address the function of the behavior.
- Change the environment when appropriate and possible.
- Recognize and modify behavioral triggers.

An individualized intervention plan is based on an understanding of the behavior in the context where it occurs. The team should identify the triggers and functions of the challenging behavior, and how consequences maintain or reinforce it. Tailor the intervention plan to fit the unique circumstances of the child and his family, and include strategies for teaching the child new skills and new prevention strategies in addition to reducing problem behavior.

Prevention and intervention strategies can be developed to make changes in the triggers, consequences, skills, and broad contextual factors of challenging behavior. Remember, the process of altering problem behavior involves change in the child's behavior with family, staff, and peers in a variety of settings. The goal of an intervention plan is to make challenging behaviors irrelevant, inefficient, and ineffective compared to prosocial behaviors. Consider the following examples:

- **Behavior:** Natalie screams when another child takes the doll that she has laid in the crib.
- **Situation:** This behavior only occurs when somebody has taken an item she has been playing with. If nobody takes the item, the screaming behavior does not occur.
- **Function:** The function of her behavior is to obtain an adult's attention to provide assistance in regaining the item.

There are some options for addressing Natalie's behavior. Her caregiver could make the behavior irrelevant. The problem behavior represents

WHEN NOTHING ELSE WORKS

an adaptation to a situation; therefore, by changing the situation, the challenging behavior no longer serves a function and becomes irrelevant. An intervention strategy such as ignoring would make Natalie's attention-motivated behavior ineffective.

Her caregiver could make the behavior inefficient. The problem behavior becomes comparatively inefficient when a more acceptable replacement behavior fulfills the same function faster and with less effort. Her caregiver could encourage Natalie to use her words to express her wants and needs, teaching her a more efficient method of getting what she wants. At first, the caregiver would need to give Natalie a script to use to protest the actions of the child who took the doll and to get help from an adult if the solution is not resolved. This prosocial behavior is more efficient because Natalie regains the baby doll more quickly.

- **Behavior:** Justin uses inappropriate language at his preschool.
- **Situation:** He uses the language when other people are around to hear him and react.
- **Function:** He is trying to obtain the attention of adults and other children in the program.

Make the behavior ineffective. Changing the consequences that follow challenging behaviors can make them ineffective at obtaining the payoff that maintained them. His caregiver can change the response of the entire class by asking them to ignore Justin's inappropriate language, making it ineffective as a means to obtain attention.

When the intervention plan addresses the function of the behavior and employs prevention and intervention strategies that make the challenging behavior irrelevant, inefficient, and ineffective, the plan will have a positive effect on the behavior.

WORKING WITH A TEAM TO ADDRESS CHALLENGING BEHAVIOR

The Division for Early Childhood (DEC) of the Council for Exceptional Children strongly believes that partnerships among families, service providers, and caregivers—in which each family's unique strengths, concerns, and responsibilities are fully recognized—are critical to the design and implementation of interventions.

175

An integral part of the team in evaluating and addressing challenging behavior, parents and family members can share information about strategies that have been tried in the past, how their child's behavior varies across settings, the effect of challenging behavior on the family, and family goals for the child's behavior. They also can implement interventions in the home and other community environments outside the school or child care setting. The level and type of family involvement should be determined by the family, based on their priorities, rather than prescribed by professionals or programs.

A coordinated effort ensures that intervention plans are acceptable to all team members. The plan must be feasible to implement within different settings and must effectively address challenging behavior as it provides support for desired behavior. A coordinated effort also facilitates shared understanding among families, teachers, and other team members about why challenging behavior is occurring and which interventions will be implemented.

Effective partnerships between families and staff do not place blame; rather, they identify strategies that match the needs of the child and provide support for appropriate behavior. Effective partnerships focus on developing strategies that build on the strengths and effective practices of team members and provide support to team members. This helps participants implement interventions appropriately and consistently. Support can be offered in a variety of ways:

- Written descriptions of intervention strategies
- Modeling
- Skill building and coaching
- Ongoing communication and team meetings
- Revisions to interventions as needed

COLLECTING DATA

Before you can develop an intervention plan, you must identify the behavior you want to modify and understand the context in which the behavior occurs. Anyone working with the child can collect data: administrators, teachers, assistants, paraprofessionals, specialists, or family members. The most important variable is that the individual must have the opportunity to observe the behavior for which that data is being collected. For example, if the behavior being observed is how long it takes the child to fall asleep on his cot during nap time, this behavior may not be appropriate for family to measure since they are not present during the nap-time routine at preschool. However, if the behavior is how long it takes the child to fall asleep at night once the bedtime routine is completed, then family members would be the appropriate individuals to collect the data.

There are two kinds of information to collect: indirect and direct observational data.

Indirect observational data: Interview family members and others who have had ongoing responsibility for supervising the child in question. Be sure that you give each stakeholder a functional description of the behavior, to be sure it is the same behavior you are observing.

Direct observational data: Determine which kinds of data you need, and select the most appropriate tool. Is it the frequency or the intensity of the behavior that has you concerned? Does the behavior seem to occur without warning? Can the behavior be redirected, or does it intensify when you intervene?

 Frequency or scatter-plot tool: If the behavior is frequent, you will want to use a *frequency* or *scatter-plot tool* (see Figure 10.1). A frequency tool is simply a record of how frequently a behavior appears during a finite period. Results are measured in terms of number of occurrences per hour. A scatter plot can help identify patterns in

Figure 10.1

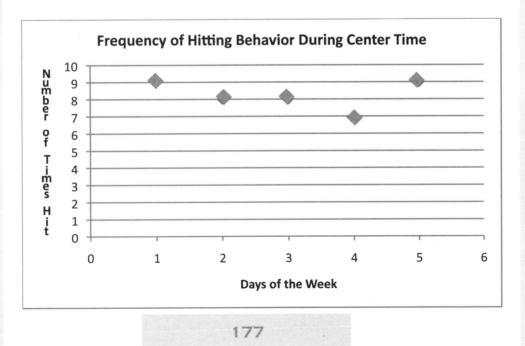

CHAPTER 10 ■ DEVELOPING AN INTERVENTION PLAN

the occurrence of behaviors. By pairing certain activities with the occurrence of behaviors, often you can identify antecedents or triggers and possibly the consequence that is reinforcing the behavior.

For data to be useful, you need to know how many times a behavior occurs within a certain time frame, such as group time. To calculate the frequency of the event, count the number of occurrences of the event within a fixed time interval, and then divide by the length of the time interval. Use these methods if the behavior has a clear beginning and end and can be counted easily, such as using obscene language or gestures. Do not use these methods if the behavior occurs so frequently that an accurate count is impossible (for example, wiggling during group time) or the behavior occurs for extended periods of time (for example, two tantrums lasting one hour each). A frequency measure should be used only when the length of observation time is consistent from day to day (for example, always two hours). Use a rate measure if the length of observation time varies from day to day (for example, one hour on Monday, two hours on Tuesday).

The rate of the behavior is calculated by counting the total number of times the behavior occurred and dividing that number by the length of time of the observation. For example, on the previous data graph, the rate of the behavior during center time would be calculated by taking the number of incidents (hitting behavior on the first day, which was nine) and dividing by the duration of the observation period (two hours). The rate of hitting behavior for the first day would be 4.5 hits per hour. The rate for the entire week would be 4.2 hits per hour.

The number of occurrences of a behavior can be easily and unobtrusively recorded using a hand tally counter; making marks on masking tape applied to clothing, a desk, or wrist; or transferring pennies, buttons, or other small objects from one pocket to another.

- **Duration measure:** If the behavior lasts a long time, you may want to use a *duration measure* (see Figure 10.2). Whereas scatter plots provide information about when the behavior happens, duration measures indicate *how long* a particular behavior tends to last, when it begins, and when it ends. Use this method if your primary concern is the length of time the child engages in the behavior and the behavior has a clear beginning and end. Do not use this method if the behavior occurs at a high frequency or the behavior starts and stops rapidly.

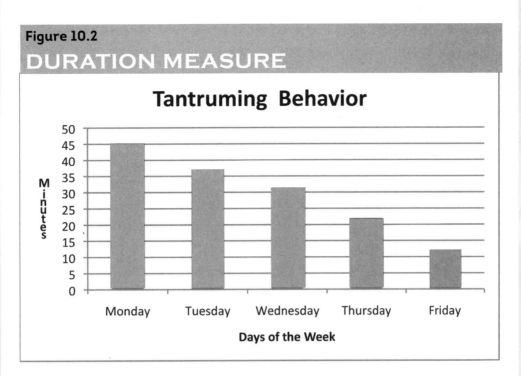

Figure 10.2

DURATION MEASURE

Tantruming Behavior

For example, use duration measures to collect data on how long a tantrum behavior occurs or how long it takes the child fall asleep during the nap-time routine.

■ **Interval data method:** An alternative to the duration measure, the *interval data method* uses observation periods divided into a number of smaller time periods or intervals (see Figure 10.3). The observer watches the student throughout each interval and then records whether or not the behavior occurred during that interval. Use this method if the behavior occurs continuously or at a high frequency. Do not use this method if the behavior is a low-frequency behavior.

For example, if the behavior to observe is hitting and the hitting occurs frequently, then an interval measure would be appropriate. However, if the behavior to observe is throwing a tantrum when a child's mother leaves, this behavior does not happen often enough to best be measured by interval recording.

Interval recording is useful for estimating the number of occurrences and/or duration of the behavior. There are two types of interval recording: partial and whole. *Partial-interval recording* indicates whether the behavior was present or absent **at any time** during the interval. The number of times the behavior occurred is not a concern. Use a data sheet divided into appropriate intervals to record occurrences of the behavior. Partial-interval recording tends to produce a slight overestimate of the presence of the target behavior and should therefore be used when the goal is to produce a behavior reduction. *Whole-interval recording* tracks the behavior that is present throughout the entire interval. This procedure tends to produce a slight underestimate of the presence of the target behavior and should be used when the goal is to produce an increase in behavior.

Both partial-interval and whole-interval recording require that someone experienced in measuring data fully attends to the child during the period being recorded. Use a stopwatch or other timing device, such as a digital kitchen timer, a pencil, and paper divided into intervals to document the occurrence of the behavior.

Figure 10.3

INTERVAL RECORDING TABLE

	:10 sec	:10 sec	:10 sec	:10 sec	:10 sec	:10 sec	+/total
Unable to remain in assigned area							
Record a (+) for occurrence and a (-) for a non-occurrence							

For whole-interval recording, mark (+) if the behavior occurs for the entire interval. In partial-interval recording, mark (+) if the behavior occurred <u>at least once</u> during the observation interval.

■ **Latency recording:** Latency recording is useful for measuring the time it takes for a child to respond to a prompt. For example, if a teacher asks a student to put an activity away, the observer would be interested in the length of time it takes for the student to comply with the request. Use this method if the opportunity and the behavior have a clear beginning and end, such as how long it takes to come to group time or to clean up the center.

Keeping data on a child's behavior can give insight into exactly what behavior is exhibited, what transpires directly prior to the behavior, and the consequences the child receives for the behavior. The easiest way to collect behavioral data is on a clipboard or notebook that is easily accessible to the adults in the program. This provides a quick means for the teacher to jot down notes about each occurrence.

The following steps will assist you in collecting data by recording the specific behavior to be observed:

1. Define the behavior that you wish to observe. Be very specific. Be sure that your definition is so narrow in scope that others would observe only what you had in mind.

2. Decide which type of behavioral recording is best suited to monitor the behavior: frequency, interval, duration, or latency.

3. Decide when you will observe the behavior. Do you want to observe the behavior in a variety of situations or just one situation, such as center time or story time?

4. Decide how long each of your observations will last. Ten to twenty minutes is usually adequate, but the more time you spend observing, the more accurate your results will be. Repeat your observations at least three more times to provide a more representative picture.

5. Observe and record the child's behavior.

6. If you use frequency recording, determine the average number of occurrences per minute, hour, or day. If you use duration recording, calculate the percentage of the total observation time during which the behavior occurred.

DEVELOPING AN INTERVENTION PLAN

Once you have observed the child and have gathered the data on her behavior, you can work with the child's family, service providers, and other caregivers to design an intervention plan. The development of an intervention plan for children must include the following factors:

1. The plan must be based on an understanding of the behavior in the context where it occurs.

2. The plan must be tailored to fit the unique circumstances of the individual child (and her family) with a consideration of all variables in the child's environment, including the unique culture of the family system.

3. The intervention plan should include strategies for teaching the child new skills in addition to reducing and preventing problem behavior.

4. The plan should be designed for implementation by family members and early childhood staff in all relevant environments.

When developing the plan, make sure that everything is spelled out clearly and specifically so that everyone involved with the child can use the interventions easily. In most circumstances, the plan should be no more than two to three pages in length. If it is much longer than that, it will be more difficult for people to remember and follow. The interventions included should be ones the team has the resources and abilities to implement. Once the team agrees on an intervention plan, everyone involved must agree to implement it consistently. If even one person feels that he is unable support the plan, it must be revisited and adapted accordingly. Inconsistent application of any intervention is likely to result in an increase in the challenging behavior or the presentation of new inappropriate behaviors.

OUTLINE FOR DEVELOPING AN INTERVENTION PLAN

Phase I: Gathering Background Information

- Compile and read the case history.
- Make observations.
- Conduct structured interviews with those who know the child best, such as parents, family members, guardian, and caregivers.

Phase II: Defining the Problem

- When does the behavior occur?
- Where does the behavior occur?
- How often does the behavior occur?
- How long does the behavior last?
- Are there any identifiable triggers?
- Are there any other factors directly related to the behavior?

Phase III: Identifying a Goal

- What you would like to see happen?

Phase IV: Attempted Interventions and Their Results

- Describe the interventions that have been tried, remembering to document how long they have been attempted and how successful they have been.

Phase V: Developing Intervention Strategies

1. Brainstorm solutions
   Professionals and family members generate a list of ways to deal with the problem behavior. Include the following factors:
   - expectations
   - environmental structuring
   - classroom intervention

WHEN NOTHING ELSE WORKS

2. Make decisions

   After generating a list of ideas, the team evaluates each solution to determine which one will be the most effective. Consider the following:

   ■ What is the likelihood that this choice will reduce the child's inappropriate behavior?

   ■ What is the likelihood that I can implement this solution in its optimal form?

3. Identify responsibilities for implementing the plan

   ■ Specify who is responsible for implementing specific portions of the plan.

   ■ Establish timelines for implementation.

Phase VI: Implementing the Intervention

Once the team develops an intervention plan, the plan must be implemented with fidelity. One of the reasons that behavior does not change is the plan not being implemented as prescribed—for example, parents need to implement certain strategies on a daily basis; however, if the strategies are not implemented as described in the plan, this may impact the fidelity of the plan and result in minimal change in behavior.

Phase VII: Evaluating and Verifying

Evaluate the plan to see if it is accomplishing the goal you have established. If the plan is effective in reducing the child's inappropriate behavior, congratulations. However, if the child's behavior does not change, you must determine the reasons why and address them by modifying the plan.

Evaluating the Effectiveness of the Intervention

Once the plan is implemented, stakeholders need to collect data to determine if the plan addresses the behavior of concern. If the data indicate a decrease in the behavior, then the plan is working and should continue to be implemented as prescribed. However, if there is no observable change in the behavior within a two- to three-week period, the team needs to reconvene and discuss why the plan is not working. The behavior may not decrease for a number of reasons, including the plan not being implemented as specified; the team has not determined the true function of the behavior; or the strategies developed do not have the desired effect on the behavior. The team needs to discuss all the possible reasons and determine what action to take.

Figure 10.4

FREQUENCY BEFORE AND AFTER INTERVENTION

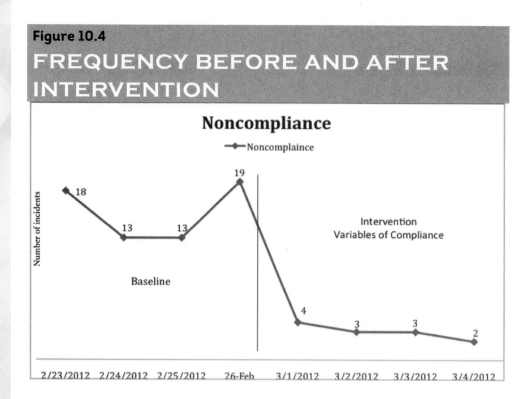

The graph in Figure 10.4 documents the noncompliant behavior exhibited by a child in a preschool program before and after an intervention is implemented. The data points on the left-hand side labeled "baseline" track the frequency of behavior on four consecutive days before the intervention was implemented. The line in the middle of the graph indicates the phase line, which denotes the move from baseline to intervention. The data points on the right side of the phase line track the frequency of the behavior for four consecutive days after the intervention had been implemented. As the graph indicates, this child's noncompliant behavior significantly decreased after the interventions were implemented. The interventions focusing on variables of compliance are discussed in Chapter 7.

Following are some sample intervention plans, along with a reproducible blank intervention plan.

INTERVENTION PLAN

CHILD'S NAME:

PROGRAM:	DATE

DESCRIPTION OF THE PROBLEM:

UNDERSTANDING THE PROBLEM:

GOALS SET:

INTERVENTIONS IMPLEMENTED AT HOME AND SCHOOL:

INTERVENTIONS IMPLEMENTED AT SCHOOL:

INTERVENTIONS IMPLEMENTED AT HOME:

SAMPLE INTERVENTION PLAN I

CHILD'S NAME: Don

PROGRAM: Happy Preschool	BIRTHDATE: 1/20/2007

INTERVENTION DATES

Date of Initiation of Intervention: 4/26/2011

Revision of Intervention: 6/14/2011

Revision of Intervention: 6/28/2011

Revision of Intervention: 7/11/2011

Revision of Intervention: 8/14/2011

Revision of Intervention: 9/10/2011

Revision of Intervention: 9/24/2011

DESCRIPTION OF THE PROBLEM

Don is noncompliant to teacher requests and classroom guidelines. He interacts negatively with peers and adults; for example, he hits other children, refuses to share toys, and runs away from the teacher. He can be unsafe during transitions to and from outdoor play.

GOALS SET:

1. When given a request or teacher directive, Don will comply.
2. Don will play and interact with peers in the classroom.
3. Don will transition to and from the playground without assistance from the educational staff.

INTERVENTION STRATEGIES

- Continue to use positive start commands, describing what you want Don to do.
- When giving directions, the educational staff should model and demonstrate what is expected of Don.
- Have Don repeat the direction or explain to the educational staff what he is expected to do, especially during transitions.
- Whenever possible, the educational staff needs to ignore defiant behavior—especially if Don is not hurting himself or others, destroying property, or being disruptive to the class.
- If Don appears to be in a negative mood, attempt to distract him into a positive mood.
- Continue to give Don choices, and help him be responsible for his behavior. Have Don demonstrate his understanding of the choices given.
- When giving Don a choice, have a logical consequence attached to it. Logical consequences can either be related corrective consequences, reparations, or immediate practice of alternative behaviors.
- Provide Don with scripts on how to enter play, and provide support for the play to continue.
- Provide scripts on how to resolve conflicts between Don and his peers.

- Since Don appears to enjoy outdoor play, sensory play, and nutritional activities, the educational staff should focus their interactions on those activities.
- Use books to help Don be aware, gain new insights, and adjust to situations and changes he may be currently facing.
- Help Don understand the feeling of disappointment when it occurs.
- If possible, extend outdoor playtime, so Don can have more positive experiences.
- Employ and follow through on natural and logical consequences, and remind Don of those consequences.
- For physically aggressive behavior, Don will not be given a warning—the consequence will occur immediately.
- When Don initially enters the room, his teacher will discuss with him what the expectations are and the schedule of the day.
- Visually post expectations, the daily schedule, and difficult transitions.
- Since Don appears to be angry and has a hard time calming himself down, use calming techniques with him:
  - Slow down and practice deep breathing, using visual cues.
  - Engage in progressive relaxation.
  - Develop calming scripts or use books as a form of calming script to help Don relax.
  - Mirror therapy—use a mirror to work on facial expressions.
  - Use therapeutic materials such as a stress ball, gel bags, and sensory materials to help Don work out his tension.
  - Develop a quiet area Don can visit to help calm him down when he is feeling anxious.
- Move his cubbie to the inside of the classroom so adults can monitor his behavior and give him the opportunity to go to his cubbie and get his sleeping bag.
- If necessary, use a transitional object to help Don transition from outside play to back inside the classroom.
- If necessary, develop a book of pictures describing the transition to and from outside play, to help Don during this difficult time.
- Educational staff needs to be aware when Don is upset and to find ways to channel his anger in an appropriate manner.
- Mother will record a few messages Don can play when he needs reassurance and support from her.
- Develop a differential reinforcement system to determine the schedule for reinforcement and type of reinforcer. A differential reinforcement system refers to the adult having a hierarchy of reinforcers to use at different times to increase the desirable behavior. For example, positive comments are always used whenever possible to reinforce the desired behavior, but social activities may be used on a more limited basis.

INTERVENTION STRATEGIES (CONT'D.)

- Remember that the reinforcer should be as natural as possible, should not take a lot of staff time, and should not cost a lot of money.
- Guidelines for reinforcement include:
    - Be descriptive: Instead of saying "great job" or "thanks," briefly describe the behavior you observed.
    - Be enthusiastic: Use tone of voice, facial expressions, and personal space to convey your enthusiasm when you deliver feedback. Show that you are paying attention to Don, that his behavior matters to you, and that you celebrate his accomplishments and effort.
    - Be positive: Positive Behavior Support programs promote a ratio of five positive statements for every correction.
    - Recognize effort: Encourage Don's efforts as well as his successes.
- Since Don likes the attention of the teacher, the instructor may use this as part of the reinforcement system.
- Since Don enjoys toy cars, they can be incorporated into the reinforcement system.
- Develop a reinforcement schedule based on Don's interests and needs, to motivate him to accomplish the behavioral goal.
- "Catch" Don exhibiting appropriate behavior, and provide him some positive attention.
- Develop a safety book for Don that will include safety expectations of the classroom, ways that Don can keep himself and the other children safe, and methods for calming himself down when he becomes upset.

EVALUATION

Don participating in small group, individual activities, and transitions

OBSERVATION

Teacher will collect frequency data on the number of times Don complies with adult requests. During transitions outside the classroom, teacher will collect data on the number of times Don safely transitions.

NEXT INTERVENTION MEETING

Friday, Oct. 19, 2011

SAMPLE INTERVENTION PLAN 2

CHILD'S NAME: Tyler

PROGRAM: Wonderful Preschool	**BIRTHDATE: 5/7/2008**

DATE OF INITIATION OF INTERVENTION

8/21/2012

DESCRIPTION OF THE PROBLEM

Tyler has exhibited inappropriate language and physical aggression consisting of hitting, biting, and scratching when he becomes angry, especially toward adults. In addition, he will cry for extended periods of time throughout the day.

GOALS SET:

1. When Tyler becomes upset, he will display or express his anger in an acceptable manner.
2. Tyler will begin to calm himself down when he becomes upset.

INTERVENTION STRATEGIES

- Educational staff models appropriate behavior.
- Educational staff removes Tyler from the situation and redirects him to another activity when he becomes upset.
- Educational staff models and assists Tyler in how to solve a problem that causes him to become angry.
- Whenever possible, the educational staff ignores tantrum behavior, especially if Tyler is not hurting himself or others, destroying property, or being disruptive to the class.
- Continue to give Tyler choices, and help him be responsible for his behavior. Have him demonstrate his understanding of the choices.
- When giving a choice, have a logical consequence attached. Logical consequences can be related corrective consequences, reparations, or immediate practice of alternative behaviors.
- Employ and follow through on natural and logical consequences, and remind Tyler of those consequences.
- For physically aggressive behavior, Tyler will not be given a warning–the consequence will occur immediately.
- As soon as Tyler enters the room, the teacher will discuss what the expectations are and the schedule for the day (especially if there are any changes for the day or week).
- Visually post expectations, the daily schedule, and difficult transitions.
- Develop a book that shows the positive things children can do with their hands.

Intervention Strategies (Cont'd.)

- Develop a book based on the format of *Brown Bear, Brown Bear, What Do You See?* by Bill Martin, Jr. and Eric Carle to assist Tyler in understanding the relationships among the individuals in his life.
- When Tyler appears to be angry and has a hard time calming himself down, use calming techniques:
  - Slow down and practice deep breathing using visual cues.
  - Engage in progressive relaxation.
  - Develop calming scripts or use books as a form of calming script to help Tyler relax.

Evaluation

Observation: The staff will track the number of incidents of frustration and anger involving kicking, hitting, pinching, and biting—and the length of the episodes—on a daily basis. In addition, the staff will track the days when Tyler sees his biological father.

Next Intervention Meeting

Oct. 16, 2012, at 2:00 p.m.

SAMPLE INTERVENTION PLAN 3

CHILD'S NAME: Janice

PROGRAM: Joyful Preschool　　　　　　　**BIRTHDATE:** 6/26/2008

DATE OF INITIATION OF INTERVENTION　　September 6, 2012

DESCRIPTION OF THE PROBLEM

Janice has a difficult time following the classroom guidelines and procedures. She requires constant attention, especially during centers, lunch, self-help, and transition times. She is more active than other children and has a difficult time concentrating on one task. She has impulsive behavior that can be hurtful to herself and others when she is angry or asked to follow rules and routines. Janice resorts to hitting, kicking, biting, and scratching when she is angry. She has run away from teachers on several occasions in the hallway, lunchroom, and restroom. In addition, Janice has run out of the classroom.

GOALS SET

1. Janice will comply with adult requests.
2. Janice will remain with the group/peers in the classroom and during transitions outside of the classroom.
3. Janice will respect the personal space of others by keeping her hands and body to herself.

INTERVENTION STRATEGIES

- The teachers have been using a reward system with Janice.
- The teachers have been in constant communication with her parents to brainstorm possible solutions.
- The teachers will assist Janice during transitions using warning time and close proximity.
- The teachers are using books and feelings posters to help Janice identify feelings and discuss appropriate behaviors.
- The teachers have used redirection and warning time to assist in behavior control.
- Mother will bring Janice into the classroom. As soon as she enters the room, teacher and mother will discuss the expectations with her, especially (following staff's request) keeping hands and body to herself and using words to express anger and frustration.
- At home, mother and father will address what he watches on television.
- At night, mother or father will tell Janice she will have a great day at school the next day and remind her to follow the expectations that have been established in the classroom.
- Mother and father will address with Janice's sibling the effect of his behavior on Janice.
- Mother and father will interact with Janice as other adults would with a typically developing four-year-old female.

- Mother and father will attempt to eliminate the wrestling that occurs between Janice and other relatives.

- When giving Janice a choice, have a logical consequence attached. Logical consequences can be related corrective consequences, reparations, or immediate practice of alternate behaviors.

- Whenever possible, the educational staff and mother/father need to ignore defiant behavior, especially if Janice is not hurting herself or others, destroying property, or being disruptive to the class.

- Because Janice engages in scratching behavior, mother and father will attempt to cut her fingernails.

- Develop a differential reinforcement system to determine the schedule of reinforcement and the type of reinforcer. Remember that the reinforcer should be as natural as possible, should not take a lot of staff time or cost a lot of money. Remember to implement the guidelines for reinforcement (be descriptive, be enthusiastic, be positive, recognize effort).

- During group experiences, Janice will sit between two students who are positive role models for her and are able to ignore her off-task behavior. In addition, she will have the opportunity to sit in a beanbag chair. Adult will redirect her to the task at hand as needed.

- To help Janice keep her hands to herself and channel her energy into more appropriate behavior, she will have the opportunity to manipulate a fidget during group experiences. The parents and teacher have provided a variety of items, and Janice will pick the one she wants to use.

- If possible, keep the classroom door closed to deter Janice from leaving the room. Install bells or other auditory devices on the door to warn the adults that the door has been opened.

- Post a stop sign on the door as a visual cue to deter Janice from leaving the room.

- Stretch colored tape across the door frame as a three-dimensional cue to prevent her from leaving the classroom.

- Place child-safety doorknobs on the front and back classroom doors, making it difficult for Janice to open the doors.

- If the above preventive strategies are not successful, with fire marshal approval, install a safety gate to prevent access to the exit.

- Continue to use positive start commands, describing what you want Janice to do.

- When giving directions, model and demonstrate what is expected of Janice.

- During transitions outside of the classroom, for Janice's safety, it is important to have her in close proximity and even hold her hand if you think she may run from you.

OBSERVATION

- Teacher will collect frequency data on the number of incidents involving physical contact (hitting, scratching, biting, kicking, or pushing) between Janice and others.
- Teacher will also collect frequency data on the number of times Janice complies with adult requests.
- During transitions outside the classroom, teacher will collect data on the number of times Janice leaves the group.

NEXT INTERVENTION MEETING

Tuesday, Sept. 12, 2012, 1:30 p.m.

References

Alberto, Paul, and Anne Troutman. 1999. *Applied Behavior Analysis for Teachers, 5th ed.* Columbus, OH: Merrill.

Anda, Robert, Vincent Felitti, John Walker, Charles Whitfield, J. Douglas Bremner, Bruce Perry, Shanta Dube, and Wayne Giles. 2006. "The Enduring Effects of Abuse and Related Adverse Experiences in Childhood: A Convergence of Evidence from Neurobiology and Epidemiology." *European Archives of Psychiatry and Clinical Neurosciences* 256(3): 174–186.

Angleitner, Jan, Alois Strelau, and Jan Strelau, eds. 1991. *Explorations in Temperament: International Perspectives on Theory and Measurement.* New York: Plenum.

Araújo, Nina, and Carol Aghayan. 2006. *Easy Songs for Smooth Transitions in the Classroom.* St. Paul, MN: Redleaf.

Aronson, Joshua, ed. *Improving Academic Achievement: Impact of Psychological Factors on Education.* San Diego, CA: Academic Press.

Bakley, Sue. 2001. "Through the Lens of Sensory Integration: A Different Way of Analyzing Challenging Behavior." *Young Children* 56(6): 70–76.

Barlow, David, Michel Hersen, and Matthew Nock. 1984. *Single-Case Experimental Designs: Strategies for Studying Behavior Change.* New York: Pergamon.

Bayat, Mojdeh, Gayle Mindes, and Sheryl Covitt. 2010. "What Does RTI (Response to Intervention) Look Like in Preschool?" *Early Childhood Education Journal* 37(6): 493–500.

Bell, Susan, Victoria Carr, Dawn Denno, Lawrence Johnson, and Louise Phillips. 2004. *Challenging Behaviors in Early Childhood Settings: Creating a Place for All Children.* Baltimore, MD: Brookes.

Benard, Bonnie. 2004. *Resiliency: What We Have Learned.* San Francisco, CA: WestEd.

Berkson, Gershon, and Megan Tupa. 2000. "Early Development of Stereotyped and Self-Injurious Behaviors." *Journal of Early Intervention,* 23(1) 1–19.

Berwick, Ann. 1994. *Aromatherapy: A Holistic Guide.* Woodbury, MN: Llewellyn.

Bierman, Karen, Celene Domitrovich, Robert Nix, Scott Gest, Janet Welsh, Mark Greenberg, Clancy Blair, Keith Nelson, and Sukhdeep Gill. 2008. "Promoting Academic and Social-Emotional School Readiness: The Head Start REDI Program." *Child Development* 79(6): 1802–1817.

Bilmes, Jenna. 2008. *Beyond Behavior Management: The Six Life Skills Children Need.* St. Paul, MN: Redleaf.

Bishop, Robin, and Martin Rimes. 2006. "Better Design for Young Children." *Early Education,* Spring. British Association for Early Childhood Education.

Blair, Kwang-Sun, John Umbreit, and Candace Bos. 1999. "Using Functional Assessment and Children's Preferences to Improve the Behavior of Young Children with Behavioral Disorders." *Behavioral Disorders* 24, 151–166.

Blakemore, Sarah-Jane, and Uta Frith. 2005. *The Learning Brain: Lessons for Education.* Malden, MA: Blackwell.

Blakemore, Sarah-Jane, Joel Winston, and Uta Frith. 2004. "Social Neuroscience: Where Are We Heading?" *Trends in Cognitive Sciences* 8(5): 216–222.

Bodrova, Elena, and Deborah Leong. 2008. "Developing Self-Regulation in Kindergarten: Can We Keep All the Crickets in the Basket?" *Young Children* 63(2): 56–58.

Bouchard, Thomas, Jr. 1994. "Genes, Environment, and Personality." *Science* 264(5166): 1700–1701.

Brackett, Marc, Susan Rivers, Sara Shiffman, Nicole Lerner, and Peter Salovey. 2006. "Relating Emotional Abilities to Social Functioning: A Comparison of Self-Report and Performance Measures of Emotional Intelligence." *Journal of Personality and Social Psychology* 91(4): 780–795.

Bradway, Deborah. 2009. "Music Therapy as a Treatment for Substance Abuse with At-Risk Children and Adolescents," Parts 1 and 2. Retrieved from http://www.remo.com/portal/hr/article?id=19 and http://www.remo.com/portal/hr/article?id=20.

Bredekamp, Sue, and Carol Copple, eds. 1997. *Developmentally Appropriate Practice in Early Childhood Programs,* rev. ed. Washington, DC: National Association for the Education of Young Children.

Breslin, Deirdre. 2005. "Children's Capacity to Develop Resiliency: How to Nurture It." *Young Children* 60(1): 47–48, 50–52.

Brickman, Nancy, and Lynn Taylor, eds. 1991. *Supporting Young Learners: Ideas for Preschool and Day Care Providers.* Ypsilanti, MI: High/Scope.

WHEN NOTHING ELSE WORKS

Briody, Jennifer, and Kathleen McGarry. 2005. "Using Social Stories to Ease Children's Transitions." *Young Children* 60(5): 38–42.

Bronson, Martha. 2000. *Self-Regulation in Early Childhood: Nature and Nurture.* New York: Guilford.

Brophy, Jere. 2000. *Teaching.* Geneva, Switzerland: International Bureau of Education.

Brown, Stuart. 2009. *Play: How It Shapes the Brain, Opens the Imagination, and Invigorates the Soul.* New York: Penguin.

Bruce, Nefertiti, and Karen Cairone. 2011. *Socially Strong, Emotionally Secure: 50 Activities to Promote Resilience in Young Children.* Silver Spring, MD: Gryphon House.

Bruno, Holly Elissa. 2008. *Leading on Purpose: Emotionally Intelligent Early Childhood Administration.* New York: McGraw-Hill.

Cacioppo, John, and Gary Berntson, eds. 2004. *Essays in Social Neuroscience.* Cambridge, MA: MIT Press.

Cameron, Judy, and W. David Pierce. 2002. *Rewards and Intrinsic Motivation: Resolving the Controversy.* Westport, CT: Bergin and Garvey.

Campbell, Susan. 1995. "Behavior Problems in Preschool Children: A Review of Recent Research." *Journal of Child Psychology and Psychiatry and Allied Disciplines* 36(1): 113–149.

Carlson, Frances. 2006. *Essential Touch: Meeting the Needs of Young Children.* Washington, DC: National Association for the Education of Young Children.

Carlson, Frances. 2011. *Big Body Play: Why Boisterous, Vigorous, and Very Physical Play Is Essential to Children's Development and Learning.* Washington, DC: National Association for the Education of Young Children.

Carr, James, and Eric Burkholder. 1998. "Creating Single-Subject Design Graphs with Microsoft Excel." *Journal of Applied Behavior Analysis* 31(2): 245–251.

Carter, Deborah, Renee Van Norman, and Claire Tredwell. 2011. "Program-Wide Positive Behavior Support in Preschool: Lessons for Getting Started." *Early Childhood Education Journal* 38(5): 349–55.

Choi, Ae-Na, Myeong Soo Lee, and Jung-Sook Lee. 2010. "Group Music Intervention Reduces Aggression and Improves Self-Esteem in Children with Highly Aggressive Behavior: A Pilot Controlled Trial." *Evidence-Based Complementary and Alternative Medicine* 7(2): 213–217.

Chong, Trevor, Ross Cunningham, Mark Williams, Nancy Kanwisher, and Jason Mattingly. 2008. "fMRI Adaptation Reveals Mirror Neurons in Human Inferior Parietal Cortex." *Current Biology* 18: 1576–1580.

Chugani, Harry T. 1998. "A critical period of brain development: Studies of cerebral glucose utilization with PET." *Preventive Medicine* 27: 184–88.

Conroy, Maureen, and Janine Stichter. 2003. "The Application of Antecedents in the Functional Assessment Process: Existing Research, Issues, and Recommendations." *Journal of Special Education* 37(1): 15–25.

Conroy, Maureen, and William Brown. 2004. "Early Identification, Prevention, and Early Intervention with Young Children at Risk for Emotional or Behavioral Disorders: Issues, Trends, and a Call for Action." *Behavioral Disorders* 29(3): 224–236.

Coon, Cheryl. 2004. *Books to Grow With: A Guide to Using the Best Children's Fiction for Everyday Issues and Tough Challenges.* Portland, OR: Lutra Press.

Copple, Carol, and Sue Bredekamp, eds. 2009. *Developmentally Appropriate Practice in Early Child¬hood Programs Serving Children from Birth through Age 8,* 3rd ed. Washington, DC: National Association for the Education of Young Children.

Cozolino, Louis. 2006. *The Neuroscience of Human Relationships: Attachment and the Developing Social Brain.* New York: W.W. Norton.

Crawford, Barbara. 2001. *The Common Sense Early-Childhood Classroom: A Practical Guide to Caring for Preschool Children.* Torrance, CA: Fearon Teacher Aids.

Curtis, Deb, and Margie Carter. 2003. *Designs for Living and Learning: Transforming Early Childhood Environments.* St. Paul, MN: Redleaf.

REFERENCES

DeMeo, William. 2003. *A Practical and Research Based Model for Identifying, Preventing, and Intervening with Behavioral Problems with Young Children.* Cincinnati, OH: Specialty Psychological Services.

Denno, Dawn, Victoria Carr, and Susan Bell. 2010. A*ddressing Challenging Behaviors in Early Childhood Settings: A Teacher's Guide.* Baltimore, MD: Brookes.

DeVries, Rheta, and Betty Zan. 2003. "When Children Make Rules." *Educational Leadership,* 61(1): 22–29.

Diamond, Marian Cleeves. 1988. *Enriching Heredity: The Impact of the Environment on the Anatomy of the Brain.* New York: Free Press.

Diffily, Deborah, and Charlotte Sassman. 2004. *Teaching Effective Classroom Routines: Establish Structure in the Classroom to Foster Children's Learning.* New York: Scholastic.

Dinstein, Ilan, Justin Gardner, Mehrdad Jazayeri, and David Heeger. 2008. "Executed and Observed Movements Have Different Distributed Representations in Human aIPS." *Journal of Neuroscience* 28(44): 11231–11239.

Durlak, Joseph, and Roger Weissberg. 2007. *The Impact of After-School Programs that Promote Personal and Social Skills.* Chicago: Collaborative for Academic, Social, and Emotional Learning.

Dweck, Carol. 2006. *Mindset: The New Psychology of Success.* New York: Ballantine.

Dweck, Carol. 2012. *Mindset: How You Can Fulfill Your Potential.* London: Constable & Robinson.

Edwards, Richard, and Donald Hodges. 2007. "Neuromusical Research: An Overview of the Literature," in *Neurosciences in Music Pedagogy.* Wilfried Gruhn and Frances Rauscher, eds. New York: Nova Biomedical Books.

Edwards, Scott, Tamsen McMahon, and Jennifer Montfort, eds. 2009. "Cognitive Neuroscience: Understanding Complex Human Behavior and the Brain." *On the Brain* 15(1).

Eide, Brock, and Fernette Eide. 2006. *The Mislabeled Child: Looking Beyond Behavior to Find the True Sources and Solutions for Children's Learning Challenges.* New York: Hyperion.

Elias, Maurice, ed. 1997. *Promoting Social and Emotional Learning: Guidelines for Educators.* Alexandria, VA: Association for Supervision and Curriculum Development.

Emerson, Eric, Sheila Barrett, Caroline Bell, Richard Cummings, Heather Hughes, Christine McCool, Sandy Toogood, and Jim Mansell. 1987. *The Special Development Team: Developing Services for People with Severe Learning Difficulties and Challenging Behaviour.* Canterbury, Kent, UK: University of Kent, Institute of Social and Applied Psychology.

Emmer, Edmund, and Laura Stough. 2001. "Classroom Management: A Critical Part of Educational Psychology, with Implications for Teacher Education." *Educational Psychologist* 36(2): 103–12.

Engler, Larry, and Carol Fijan. 1997. *Making Puppets Come Alive: How to Learn and Teach Hand Puppetry.* Mineola, NY: Dover.

Epstein, Ann. 2009. *Me, You, Us: Social-Emotional Learning in Preschool.* Ypsilanti, Ml: High/Scope.

Erikson, Erik. 1963. *Childhood and Society,* 2nd ed. New York: W. W. Norton.

Evans, Betsy. 2007. "I Know What's Next!" *Preschool Transitions without Tears or Turmoil.* Ypsilanti, MI: High/Scope.

Fantuzzo, John, Rebecca Bulotsky-Shearer, Paul McDermott, Christine McWayne, Douglas Frye, and Staci Perlman. 2007. "Investigation of Dimensions of Social-Emotional Classroom Behavior and School Readiness for Low-Income Urban Preschool Children." *School Psychology Review* 36(1): 44–62.

Flicker, Eileen, and Janet Hoffman. 2006. *Guiding Children's Behavior: Developmental Discipline in the Classroom.* New York: Teachers College Press.

Fogel, Alan, Barbara King, and Stuart Shanker, eds. 2008. *Human Development in the Twenty-First Century.* Cambridge, UK: Cambridge University Press.

Fox, Lise, Glen Dunlap, Mary Louise Hemmeter, Gail Joseph, and Phillip Strain. 2003. "The Teaching Pyramid: A Model for Supporting Social Competence and Preventing Challenging Behavior in Young Children." *Young Children* 58(4): 48–52.

Fox, Lise, and Rochelle Lentini. 2006. "'You Got It!' Teaching Social and Emotional Skills." *Young Children* 61(6): 36–42.

Frey, Scott, and Valerie Gerry. 2006. "Modulation of Neural Activity During Observational Learning of Actions and Their Sequential Orders." *Journal of Neuroscience* 26(51): 13194–13201.

Galinsky, Ellen. 2010. *Mind in the Making: The Seven Essential Life Skills Every Child Needs.* New York: HarperCollins.

Gardner, Howard. 1983. *Frames of Mind: The Theory of Multiple Intelligences.* New York: Basic Books.

Gartrell, Dan. 2003. *The Power of Guidance: Teaching Social-Emotional Skills in Early Childhood Classrooms.* Belmont, CA: Wadsworth.

Gartrell, Dan. 2011. A *Guidance Approach for the Encouraging Classroom,* 5th ed. Belmont, CA: Wadsworth.

Geake, John. 2009. *The Brain at School: Educational Neuroscience in the Classroom.* Maidenhead, Berkshire, UK: Open University Press.

Gilkey, Roderick, Ricardo Caceda, and Clinton Kilts. 2010. "When Emotional Reasoning Trumps IQ." *Harvard Business Review* 88: 27

Gillespie, Linda, and Nancy Seibel. 2006. "Self-Regulation: A Cornerstone of Early Childhood Development." *Young Children* 61(4): 34–39.

Gilliam, Walter. 2005. *Prekindergarteners Left Behind: Expulsion Rates in State Prekindergarten Systems.* New Haven, CT: Yale University Child Study Center.

Gladwell, Malcolm. 2005. *Blink: The Power of Thinking without Thinking.* 2nd ed. New York: Little, Brown.

Glasser, William. 2011. *Choice Theory: A New Psychology of Personal Freedom.* New York: HarperCollins.

Goldstein, Sam. 1995. *Understanding and Managing Children's Classroom Behavior.* New York: John Wiley and Sons.

Goleman, Daniel. 1995. *Emotional Intelligence.* New York: Bantam.

Goleman, Daniel. 1998. *Working with Emotional Intelligence.* New York: Bantam.

Goleman, Daniel. 2006. *Social Intelligence: The New Science of Human Relationships.* New York: Bantam.

Good, Thomas, and Jere Brophy. 2000. *Looking in Classrooms,* 8th ed. New York: Allyn and Bacon.

Gordon, Thomas. 2003. *Teacher Effectiveness Training.* New York: Three Rivers.

Gossen, Diane. 1996. *Restitution: Restructuring School Discipline.* Chapel Hill, NC: New View.

Graybiel, Ann. 2008. "Habits, Rituals, and the Evaluative Brain." *Annual Review of Neuroscience* 31: 359–387.

Greenman, Jim. 1988. *Caring Spaces, Learning Places: Children's Environments that Work.* Redmond, WA: Exchange Press.

Greenough, William. 1987. In Norman Krasnegor, Elliot Blass, Myron Hofer, and William P. Smotherman (eds.). *Perinatal Development: A Psychobiological Perspective.* 195–221. London: Academic Press.

Guardino, Caroline and Elizabeth Fullerton. 2010. "Changing Behaviors by Changing the Classroom Environment." *Teaching Exceptional Children,* 42(6): 8-13.

Gunnar, Megan, Adriana Herrera, and Camilia Hostinar. 2009. "Stress and Early Brain Development." *Encyclopedia on Early Childhood Development.* Montreal: Centre of Excellence for Early Childhood Development.

Gunnar, Megan, and Karina Quevedo. 2007. "Early Care Experiences and HPA Axis Regulation in Children: A Mechanism for Later Trauma Vulnerability." *Progress in Brain Research: Stress Hormones and Post Traumatic Stress Disorder* 167: 137–149. Amsterdam: Elsevier.

Halfon, Neal, Ericka Shulman, and Miles Hochstein. 2001. *Brain Development in Early Childhood: Building Community Systems for Young Children.* Los Angeles: UCLA Center for Healthier Children, Families, and Communities.

Hamre, Bridget, and Robert Pianta. 2005. "Can Instructional and Emotional Support in the First-Grade Classroom Make a Difference for Children at Risk of School Failure?" *Child Development* 76(5): 949–967.

Hanlon, Grace. 2004. *Challenging Behaviors in Young Children: Techniques and Solutions.* DVD. Fair Haven, NJ: Edvantage Media.

Harrower, Joshua, Lise Fox, Glen Dunlap, and Don Kincaid. 2000. "Functional Assessment and Comprehensive Early Intervention." *Exceptionality* 8(3): 189–204.

Havener LeAnn, Lisa Gentes, Barbara Thaler, Mary Megel, Mara Baun, Frank Driscoll, Soraya Beiraghi, and Ngeeta Agrawal. 2001. "The Effects of a Companion Animal on Distress in Children Undergoing Dental Procedures." *Issues in Comprehensive Pediatric Nursing* 24(2): 137–152.

Hay, Louise, and Kristina Tracy. 2008. *I Think, I Am! Teaching Kids the Power of Affirmations.* New York: Hay House.

197

REFERENCES

Hemmeter, Mary Louise, Michaelene Ostrosky, Kathleen Artman, and Kiersten Kinder. 2008. "Moving Right Along: Planning Transitions to Prevent Challenging Behavior." *Young Children* 63(3): 18–25.

Henthorne, Mary, Nola Larson, and Ruth Chvojicek. 2000. *Transition Magician 2: More Strategies for Guiding Young Children in Early Childhood Programs.* St. Paul, MN: Redleaf.

Hester, Peggy, Heather Baltodano, Jo Hendrickson, Stephen Tonelson, Maureen Conroy, and Robert Gable. 2004. "Lessons Learned from Research on Early Intervention: What Teachers Can Do to Prevent Children's Behavior Problems." *Preventing School Failure* 49(1): 5–10.

Hewitt, Deborah. 2002. *So This Is Normal Too? Teachers and Parents Working Out Developmental Issues in Young Children.* St. Paul, MN: Redleaf.

Hirsh-Pasek, Kathryn, and John Bruer. 2007. "The Brain/Education Barrier." *Science* 317(5843): 1293.

Horn, Eva, and Hazel Jones, eds. 2006. *Supporting Social Emotional Development in Young Children.* Missoula, MT: Division for Early Childhood.

Hunt, Tamara, and Nancy Renfro. 1982. *Puppetry in Early Childhood Education.* Austin, TX: Nancy Renfro Studios.

Hyson, Marilou. 2002. "Emotional Development and School Readiness." *Young Children* 57(6): 76–78.

Hyson, Marilou. 2008. *Enthusiastic and Engaged Learners: Approaches to Learning in the Early Childhood Classroom.* New York: Teachers College Press.

Iacoboni, Marco, Istvan Molnar-Szakacs, Vittorio Gallese, Giovanni Buccino, John Mazziotta, and Giacomo Rizzolatti. 2005. "Grasping the Intentions of Others with One's Own Mirror Neuron System." *Public Library of Science Biology* 3(3): 529–535.

Isbell, Rebecca, and Betty Exelby. 2001. *Early Learning Environments that Work.* Beltsville, MD: Gryphon House.

Jalongo, Mary, ed. 2004. *The World's Children and Their Companion Animals: Developmental and Educational Significance of the Child/Pet Bond.* Olney, MD: Association for Childhood Education International.

Jenkins, Peggy. 2010. *The Joyful Child: A Sourcebook of Activities and Ideas for Releasing Children's Natural Joy,* 3rd ed. Santa Rosa, CA: Aslan.

Jervis, Kathe, and Barbara Polland. 2007. *Separation: Supporting Children in Their Preschool Transitions,* rev. ed. Washington, DC: National Association for the Education of Young Children.

Johnson, Denise. 2009. *The Joy of Children's Literature.* Boston: Harcourt.

Jolivette, Kristine, and Elizabeth Steed. 2010. "Classroom Management Strategies for Young Children with Challenging Behavior within Early Child¬hood Settings." *NHSA Dialog* 13(3): 198–213.

Jones, Nancy. 2008. "2, 4, or 6? Grouping Children to Promote Social and Emotional Development." *Young Children* 63(3): 34–39.

Kaiser, Barbara, and Judy Rasminsky. 2011. *Challenging Behavior in Young Children: Understanding, Preventing, and Responding Effectively,* 3rd ed. Upper Saddle River, NJ: Pearson.

Kelner, Lenore. 1993. *The Creative Classroom: A Guide for Using Creative Drama in the Classroom.* Portsmouth, NH: Heinemann.

Kennedy, Craig. 2005. *Single-Case Designs for Educational Research.* Boston, MA: Allyn and Bacon.

Keogh, Barbara. 2003. *Temperament in the Classroom: Understanding Individual Differences.* Baltimore, MD: Brookes.

Kersey, Katharine. 2006. *A Guide to Positive Discipline: The Facilitator's Guide.* Norfolk, VA: Old Dominion University Child Study Center.

Klein, Raymond, David Pilon, Susan Prosser, and David Shannahoff-Khalsa. 1986. "Nasal Airflow Asymmetries and Human Performance." *Biological Psychology* 23(2): 127–137.

Knudsen, Eric. 2004. "Sensitive Periods in the Development of the Brain and Behavior." *Journal of Cognitive Neuroscience* 16(8): 1412–1425.

Koegel, Lynn, Robert Koegel, and Glen Dunlap, eds. 1996. *Positive Behavioral Support: Including People with Difficult Behavior in the Community.* Baltimore, MD: Brookes.

Kohn, Alfie. 1996. *Beyond Discipline: From Compliance to Community.* Alexandria, VA: Association for Supervision and Curriculum Development.

WHEN NOTHING ELSE WORKS

Kohn, Alfie. 1999. *Punished by Rewards: The Trouble with Gold Stars, Incentive Plans, A's, Praise, and Other Bribes.* Boston: Houghton Mifflin.

Kohn, Alfie. 2006. *Beyond Discipline: From Compliance to Community,* 2nd ed. Alexandria, VA: Association for Supervision and Curriculum Development.

Koneya, Mele. 1976. *Louder than Words: Nonverbal Communication.* Indianapolis, IN: Merrill.

Kotulak, Ronald. 1998. "Inside the Brain: Revolutionary Discoveries of How the Mind Works." *Preventive Medicine,* 27(2): 246–247.

Kranowitz, Carol. 1998. *The Out-of-Sync Child: Recognizing and Coping with Sensory Integration Dysfunction.* New York: Perigee.

Kremenitzer, Janet, and Regina Miller. 2008. "Are You a Highly Qualified, Emotionally Intelligent Early Childhood Educator?" *Young Children* 63(4): 106–112.

Kristal, Jan. 2005. *The Temperament Perspective: Working with Children's Behavioral Styles.* Baltimore, MD: Brookes.

Kurtz, Patricia, Michelle Chin, John Huete, Rachel Tarbox, Julia O'Connor, Theodosia Paclawskyj, and Karena Rush. 2003. "Functional Analysis and Treatment of Self-Injurious Behavior in Young Children: A Summary of 30 Cases." *Journal of Applied Behavior Analysis* 36(2): 205–219.

LaBerge, D. 1995. *Attentional Processing: The Brain's Art of Mindfulness.* Cambridge, MA: Harvard University Press.

Lane, Kathleen, Tina Stanton-Chapman, Kristen Jamison, and Andrea Phillips. 2007. "Teacher and Parent Expectations of Preschoolers' Behavior: Social Skills Necessary for Success." *Topics in Early Childhood Special Education* 27(2): 86–97.

LeBel, Teresa, and Sandra Chafouleas. 2010. "Promoting Prosocial Behavior in Preschool: A Review of Effective Intervention Supports." *School Psychology Forum* 4(2): 25–38.

LeDoux Joseph E. 1994. "Emotion, Memory and the Brain." *Scientific American* 270(6): 32–39.

Lewis, Michael, and Carolyn Saarni, eds. 1985. *The Socialization of Emotions.* New York: Springer.

Lexmond, Jen, and Richard Reeves. 2009. *Building Character: Parents Are the Principal Architects of a Fairer Society.* London: DEMOS.

Lickona, Thomas, Ruth Nickse, David Young, and Jessie Adams, eds. 1973. *Open Education: Increasing Alternatives for Teachers and Children.* Cortland, NY: Open Education Foundation, State University of New York.

Loomis, Catherine, and Jane Wagner. 2005. "A Different Look at Challenging Behavior." *Young Children* 60(2): 94–99.

Losada, Marcial, and Emily Heaphy. 2004. "The Role of Positivity and Connectivity in the Performance of Business Teams: A Nonlinear Dynamics Model." *American Behavioral Scientist* 47(6): 740–765.

Lucyshyn, Joseph, Glen Dunlap, and Richard Albin, eds. 2002. *Families and Positive Behavior Support: Addressing Problem Behaviors in Family Contexts.* Baltimore, MD: Brookes.

Machado, Jeanne. 2007. *Early Childhood Experiences in Language Arts: Early Literacy.* Independence, KY: Thomson Delmar Learning.

Malenfant, Nicole. 2006. *Routines and Transitions: A Guide for Early Childhood Professionals.* St. Paul, MN: Redleaf.

Maltz, Maxwell. 1989. *Psycho-Cybernetics: A New Way to Get More Living Out of Life.* New York: Pocket Books.

Marion, Marian. 2011. *Guidance of Young Children,* 8th ed. Boston: Pearson-Prentice Hall.

Maslow, Abraham. 1999. *Toward a Psychology of Being,* 3rd ed. New York: John Wiley and Sons.

Masterson, Marie. 2008. "The Impact of the 101s: A Guide to Positive Discipline Training on Teacher Interaction Practices, Attitudes, and Prosocial Skill Outcomes in Preschool Classrooms." PhD diss. Norfolk, VA: Old Dominion University.

McCloud, Carol. 2006. *Have You Filled a Bucket Today? A Guide to Daily Happiness for Kids.* Northville, MI: Nelson Publishing and Marketing.

McCraty, Rollin, Mike Atkinson, and Raymond Bradley. 2004. "Electrophysiological Evidence of Intuition: Part 2. A System-Wide Process?" *The Journal of Alternative and Complementary Medicine* 10(2): 325–336.

McGann, Jayma, and Patricia Clark. 2007. "Fostering Positive Transitions for School Success." *Beyond the Journal—Young Children on the Web.* www.journal.naeyc. org/btj/200711.

REFERENCES

McGue, Matt, and Thomas Bouchard, Jr. 1998. "Genetic and Environmental Influences on Human Behavioral Differences." *Annual Review of Neuroscience* 21: 1–24.

McLaren, Elizabeth, and C. Michael Nelson. 2009. "Using Functional Behavior Assessment to Develop Behavior Interventions for Students in Head Start." *Journal of Positive Behavior Interventions* 11(1): 3–21.

Miller, David, and Kristin Sawka-Miller. 2007. "The Third Pillar: Linking Positive Psychology and School-Wide Positive Behavior Support." *School Psychology Forum* 2(1): 26–38.

Miller, Karen. 2005. *Simple Transitions for Infants and Toddlers.* Beltsville, MD: Gryphon House.

Mindess, Mary, Min-hua Chen, and Ronda Brenner. 2008. "Social-Emotional Learning in the Primary Curriculum." *Young Children* 63(6): 56–60.

Moravcik, Eva. 2000. "Music All the Livelong Day." *Young Children* 55(4): 27–29.

Nagengast, Sunny, Mara Baun, Mary Megel, and Michael Leibowitz. 1997. "The Effects of the Presence of a Companion Animal on Physiological Arousal and Behavioral Distress in Children During a Physical Examination." *Journal of Pediatric Nursing* 12(6): 323–330.

National Association for the Education of Young Children and National Association of Early Childhood Specialists in State Departments of Education. 2002. *Early Learning Standards: Creating the Conditions for Success.* Joint position statement. Washington, DC: NAEYC, NAECS-SDE.

National Institute of Child Health and Human Development Early Child Care Research Network. 2005. "Duration and Developmental Timing of Poverty and Children's Cognitive and Social Development from Birth through Third Grade." *Child Development* 76(4): 795–810.

National Scientific Council on the Developing Child. 2004. *Children's Emotional Development Is Built into the Architecture of Their Brain: Working Paper No. 2.* Retrieved from http://developingchild.harvard.edu.

National Scientific Council on the Developing Child. 2004. *Young Children Develop in an Environment of Relationships: Working Paper No. 1.* Retrieved from http://developingchild.harvard.edu.

National Scientific Council on the Developing Child. 2005. *Excessive Stress Disrupts the Architecture of the Developing Brain: Working Paper No. 3.* Retrieved from http://developingchild.harvard.edu.

National Scientific Council on the Developing Child. 2006. *Early Exposure to Toxic Substances Damages Brain Architecture: Working Paper No. 4.* Retrieved from http://developingchild.harvard.edu.

Olds, Anita. 2000. *Child Care Design Guide.* New York: McGraw-Hill.

Ostrosky, Michaelene, E. Y. Jung, Mary Louise Hemmeter, D. Thomas. 2003. *Helping Children Make Transitions between Activities.* Champaign, IL: Center on the Social and Emotional Foundations for Early Learning, University of Illinois at Urbana-Champaign.

Ostrosky, Michaelene, E. Y. Jung, Mary Louise Hemmeter, and D. Thomas. 2003. *Helping Children Understand Routines and Schedules.* Champaign, IL: Center on the Social and Emotional Foundations for Early Learning, University of Illinois at Urbana-Champaign.

Ostrosky, Michaelene, and Hedda Meadan. 2010. "Helping Children Play and Learn Together." *Young Children* 65(1): 104–110.

Payne, Linda, Terrance Scott, and Maureen Conroy. 2007. "A School-Based Examination of the Efficacy of Function-Based Intervention." *Behavioral Disorders* 32(3): 158–174.

Perry, Bruce. 2001 *Violence and Childhood: How Persisting Fear Can Alter the Developing Child's Brain.* Retrieved from www.childtrauma.org/ctamaterials/Vio_child.asp.

Piaget, Jean. 1985. *Equilibration of Cognitive Structures.* Chicago: University of Chicago Press.

Pierce, W. David, Judy Cameron, Katherine Banko, and Silvia So. 2003. "Positive Effects of Rewards and Performance Standards on Intrinsic Motivation." *Psychological Record* 53(4): 561–579.

Powell, Diane, Glen Dunlap, and Lise Fox. 2006. "Prevention and Intervention for the Challenging Behaviors of Toddlers and Preschoolers." *Infants and Young Children* 19(1): 25–35.

Qi, Cathy, and Ann Kaiser. 2003. "Behavior Problems of Preschool Children from Low-Income Families: Review of the Literature." *Topics in Early Childhood Special Education* 23(4): 188–216.

Quesenberry, Amanda, Mary Louise Hemmeter, and Michaelene Ostrosky. 2011. "Addressing Challenging Behaviors in Head Start: A Closer Look at Program Policies and Procedures." *Topics in Early Childhood Special Education* 30(4): 209–220.

Quin, Caitriona, and Scott Tawse, eds. 2009. *Handbook of Aggressive Behavior Research.* Hauppauge, NY: Nova Science Publishers.

Quinn, Mary, David Osher, Catherine Hoffman, and Tom Hanley. 1998. *Safe, Drug-Free, and Effective Schools for All Students: What Works!* Washington, DC: Center for Effective Collaboration and Practice. American Institutes for Research.

Ratcliff, Nancy. 2001. "Use the Environment to Prevent Discipline Problems and Support Learning." *Young Children* 56(5): 84–88.

Raver, Cybele, and Jane Knitzer. 2002. *Ready to Enter: What Research Tells Policymakers about Strategies to Promote Social and Emotional School Readiness among Three- and Four-Year-Old Children.* New York: National Center for Children in Poverty, Mailman School of Public Health, Columbia University.

Raver, Cybele, Stephanie Jones, Christine Li-Grining, Molly Metzger, Kina Champion, and Latriese Sardin. 2008. "Improving Preschool Classroom Processes: Preliminary Findings from a Randomized Trial Implemented in Head Start Settings." *Early Childhood Research Quarterly* 23(1): 10–26.

Repp, Alan, and Robert Horner, eds. 1999. *Functional Analysis of Problem Behavior: From Effective Assessment to Effective Support.* Belmont, CA: Wadsworth.

Rhine, Ray, ed. *Making Schools More Effective.* New York: Academic Press.

Riley, Dave, Robert San Juan, Joan Klinkner, and Ann Ramminger. 2008. *Social and Emotional Development: Connecting Science and Practice in Early Childhood Settings.* St. Paul, MN: Redleaf.

Robson, Sue. 2010. "Self-Regulation and Metacognition in Young Children's Self-Initiated Play and Reflective Dialogue." *International Journal of Early Years Education* 18(3): 227–241.

Rotz, Roland, and Sarah Wright. 2005. *Fidget to Focus: Outwit Your Boredom: Sensory Strategies for Living with ADD.* Bloomington, IN: iUniverse.

Ruth, Linda. 2000. *Design Standards for Children's Environments.* Portland, OR: McGraw-Hill.

Salovey, Peter, Marc Brackett, and John Mayer, eds. 2004. *Emotional Intelligence: Key Readings on the Mayer and Salovey Model.* Port Chester, NY: Dude Press.

Salovey, Peter, and Daisy Grewal. 2005. "The Science of Emotional Intelligence." *Current Directions in Psychological Science* 14(6): 281–285.

Sandall, Susan, Mary Louise Hemmeter, Barbara Smith, and Mary McLean. 2005. *DEC Recommended Practices: A Comprehensive Guide for Practical Application.* Longmont, CO: Sopris West.

Sandall, Susan, and Michaelene Ostrosky, eds. 1999. *Young Exceptional Children: Practical Ideas for Addressing Challenging Behaviors.* Longmont, CO: Sopris West.

Sansone, Carol, and Judith Harackiewicz, eds. 2000. *Intrinsic and Extrinsic Motivation: The Search for Optimal Motivation and Performance.* San Diego, CA: Academic Press.

Sausser, Shannon, and Raymond Waller. 2006. "A Model for Music Therapy with Students with Emotional and Behavioral Disorders." *Arts in Psychotherapy* 33(1): 1–10.

Schellenberg, Glenn. 2004. "Music Lessons Enhance IQ." *Psychological Science* 15(8): 511–514.

Selman. Robert. 2003. *The Promotion of Social Awareness: Powerful Lessons from the Partnership of Developmental Theory and Classroom Practice.* New York: Russell Sage Foundation.

REFERENCES

Serna, Loretta, Elizabeth Nielsen, Katina Lambros, and Steven Forness. 2000. "Primary Prevention with Children at Risk for Emotional or Behavioral Disorders: Data on a Universal Intervention for Head Start Classrooms." *Behavioral Disorders* 26(1): 70–84.

Shepherd, Terry, and Janice Koberstein. 1989. "Books, Puppets, and Sharing: Teaching Preschool Children to Share." *Psychology in the Schools* 26(3): 311–316.

Shonkoff, Jack, and Samuel Meisels, eds. 2000. *Handbook of Early Childhood Intervention.* New York: Cambridge University Press.

Shonkoff, Jack, and Deborah Phillips, eds. 2000. *From Neurons to Neighborhoods: The Science of Early Childhood Development.* Report of the National Research Council and Institute of Medicine, Board on Children, Youth, and Families. Washington, DC: National Academies Press.

Silberman, Mel. 1996. *Active Learning: 101 Strategies to Teach Any Subject.* Boston: Allyn and Bacon.

Sipe, Lawrence. 2007. *Storytime: Young Children's Literary Understanding in the Classroom.* New York: Teachers College Press.

Smith, Barbara, and Lise Fox. 2003. *Systems of Service Delivery: A Synthesis of Evidence Relevant to Young Children at Risk of or Who Have Challenging Behavior.* Tampa, FL: University of South Florida, Center for Evidence-Based Practice, Young Children with Challenging Behavior.

Smith, Bradley, and Adam Smith. 2005. *101 Learning and Transition Activities.* Belmont, CA: Wadsworth.

Smith, Connie. 2008. *Behavioral Challenges in Early Childhood Settings.* St. Paul, MN: Redleaf.

Stormont, Melissa, Timothy Lewis, and Rebecca Beckner. 2005. "Positive Behavior Support Systems: Applying Key Features in Preschool Settings." *Teaching Exceptional Children* 37(6): 42–49.

Strain, Phillip, and Matthew Timm. 2001. "Remediation and Prevention of Aggression: An Evaluation of the Regional Intervention Program over a Quarter Century." *Behavioral Disorders* 26(4): 297–313.

Taylor, Jill. 2008. *My Stroke of Insight: A Brain Scientist's Personal Journey.* New York: Viking-Penguin.

Thomas, Alexander, and Stella Chess. 1977. *Temperament and Development.* New York: Brunner-Routledge.

Tiger, Jeffrey, Gregory Hanley, and Emma Hernandez. 2006. "An Evaluation of the Value of Choice with Preschool Children." *Journal of Applied Behavior Analysis* 39(1): 1–16.

Timm, Matthew, and Sharon Doubet. 2008. *Acknowledging Positive Behavior: What Works Brief #22.* Nashville, TN: Center on the Social and Emotional Foundations for Early Learning.

Tokuhama-Espinosa, Tracey. 2010. *The New Science of Teaching and Learning: Using the Best of Mind, Brain, and Education Science in the Classroom.* New York: Teachers College Press.

Tremblay, Richard, Ronald Barr, Ray Peters, and Michel Boivin, eds. *Encyclopedia on Early Childhood Development.* Montreal: Centre of Excellence for Early Childhood Development. http://www.child-encyclopedia.com.

Tremblay, Richard, Daniel Nagin, Jean Séguin, Mark Zoccolillo, Philip Zelazo, Michel Boivin, Daniel Pérusse, and Christa Japel. 2004. "Physical Aggression during Early Childhood: Trajectories and Predictors." *Pediatrics* 114(1): e43–e50.

Turecki, Stanley. 1985. *The Difficult Child.* New York: Bantam Books.

Turner, Thomas. 2003. "Puppets to Put the Whole World in Their Hands." *International Journal of Social Education* 18(1): 35–45.

Vallotton, Claire, and Catherine Ayoub. 2011. "Use Your Words: The Role of Language in the Development of Toddlers' Self-Regulation." *Early Childhood Research Quarterly* 26(2): 169–181.

Vincent, Jean-Didier. 1990. *The Biology of Emotions.* Cambridge, Mass.: Basil Blackwell.

Visser, Coert. 2010. "Self-Determination Theory Meets Solution Focused Change: Autonomy, Competence, and Relatedness Support in Action." *InterAction: The Journal of Solution Focus in Organizations* 2(1): 7–26.

Watkins, Gwendolyn. 1997. "Music Therapy: Proposed Physiological Mechanisms and Clinical Implications." *Clinical Nurse Specialist* 11(2): 43–50.

Werner, Emmy. 1984. "Resilient Children." *Young Children* 40(1): 68–72.

Werner, Emmy, and Ruth Smith. 1989. *Vulnerable but Invincible: A Longitudinal Study of Resilient Children and Youth,* 3rd ed. New York: Adams, Bannister, and Cox.

Werner, Emmy, and Ruth Smith. 1992. *Overcoming the Odds: High Risk Children from Birth to Adulthood.* Ithaca, NY: Cornell University Press.

Whittaker, Jessica, and Brenda Harden. 2010. "Beyond ABCs and 123s: Enhancing Teacher-Child Relationship Quality to Promote Children's Behavioral Development." *NHSA Dialog* 13(3): 185-191.

Wien, Carol Anne. 2004. "From Policing to Participation: Overturning the Rules and Creating Amiable Classrooms." *Young Children,* 59(1): 34-40.

Willis, Clarissa. 2009. *Creating Inclusive Learning Environments for Young Children: What to Do on Monday Morning.* Thousand Oaks, CA: Corwin Press.

Wolfe, Patricia. 2001. *Brain Matters: Translating Research into Classroom Practice.* Alexandria, VA: ASCD Books.

Wood, David, Linnet McMahon, and Yvonne Cranstoun. 1980. *Working with Under Fives.* Ypsilanti, MI: High/Scope.

Worwood, Valerie. 2000. *Aromatherapy for the Healthy Child: More than 300 Natural, Nontoxic, and Fragrant Essential Oil Blends.* Novato, CA: New World Library.

Zaghlawan, Hasan, and Michaelene Ostrosky. 2011. "Circle Time: An Exploratory Study of Activities and Challenging Behavior in Head Start Classrooms." *Early Childhood Education Journal* 38(6): 439-448.

WEB RESOURCES

Center on the Social and Emotional Foundations for Early Learning (CSEFEL) focuses on promoting the social-emotional development and school readiness of children from birth through age five. The website offers resources in English and Spanish for families, trainers, teachers, and caregivers. It also includes training modules about infants, toddlers, and preschoolers, and a module for parents. http://csefel.vanderbilt.edu

Devereux Early Childhood Initiative (DECI) promotes young children's social and emotional development, resilience, and skills for school success by establishing partnerships among early childhood educators, mental health professionals, and families. DECI offers training for practitioners and parents and an assessment program for infants, toddlers, and preschool children. www.centerforresilientchildren.org

Frank Porter Graham Early Childhood Development Center focuses on sharing knowledge that enhances child development and family wellness. www.fpg.unc.edu

Technical Assistance Center on Social Emotional Intervention for Young Children (TACSEI) creates free, research-based resources to help parents, caregivers, administrators, and policy makers apply best practices when working with children who have or are at risk for delays or disabilities. The website includes a glossary of terms, briefs on systems and procedures, and related links. www.challengingbehavior.org

WEBSITES OFFERING BOOK SUGGESTIONS FOR HELPING CHILDREN WITH SOCIAL AND EMOTIONAL CONCERNS

American Psychological Association, Magination Press
> http://www.apa.org/pubs/magination/index.aspx

Bibliotherapy Booklists: Helping Young Childen Cope in Today's World
> Booklists on more than 35 important topics, prepared by the Carnegie Library of Pittsburgh. http://clpgh.org/research/parentseducators/parents/bibliotherapy/

Children's Picture Book Database at Miami University
> Miami University of Ohio produces a useful reource for bibliotherapeutic types of picture books on many topics. http://www.lib.muohio.edu/pictbks/

Library Booklists
> A compilation of links to booklists on topics ranging from bullying to sleep issues to substance abuse, as well as books supporting character education. http://librarybooklists.org/fiction/children/jidex.htm

WHEN NOTHING ELSE WORKS

INDEX

WHEN NOTHING ELSE WORKS

INDEX

WHEN NOTHING ELSE WORKS